December 1st

The History of Christmas

How did it all begin?

Across the globe, December is a magical month full of joyous celebrations. Christmas is a time for family and love. It is a time for peace and goodwill to all mankind. Christmas is a time for reflection and a time for hope. It's the only time of the year when you can see flying reindeer and spread Christmas cheer.

The true origins of the Christmas season that are celebrated today come from ancient winter celebrations. The Winter Solstice was celebrated in December. December 21st marks the first day of winter and the shortest day of the year. The Winter Solstice was a time to celebrate light and birth. It was a time to celebrate the fall harvest. There wasn't a lot of work to be done with the harvest season over. Families had time to gather and relax with good food, drink, and friendship. It was a time to celebrate the longer days ahead.

In Scandinavia, the Norse celebrated Yule. Fathers and sons would gather large logs to burn. People would gather for good food and drink while they watched the logs burn. Some of the logs would burn for as long as twelve days. The Norse people believed that each spark from the fire represented the birth of a new calf or pig in the year to come.

In Europe, the end of December was the perfect time for a celebration. Most of the cattle had been slaughtered, and the harvest was done. The Europeans had time to gather and celebrate. Most of the wine and beer was ready for drinking. Eat, drink, and be merry.

In Germany, the Germans honoured the Pagan God Odin during the Winter Solstice. The Germans believed Odin watched them and that he had the power to decide who would prosper and who would perish. Many Germans stayed indoors during the winter months in fear of Odin's powers.

In Rome, winter was not as harsh as it was in other parts of the world. The Romans celebrated the Holiday of Saturnalia. During this holiday, the Romans honoured Saturn, the God of agriculture. Saturnalia would begin the week before the Winter Solstice, and the celebrations would continue for a month. Food and drink were plentiful during the celebrations. The Roman social order was reversed. For an entire month, slaves would become masters. The peasants became the commanders. All businesses, schools, and government offices were closed. The Holiday of Saturnalia was a holiday for the entire colony to celebrate.

In the early days of Christianity, Easter was the biggest holiday celebrated. In ancient times, people only celebrated the death of saints, not their births. In the fourth century, people decided to mark the birth of Christ as a holiday. Puritans did not observe the birth of Christ as a holiday because the Bible does not state the date that Christ was born.

Susan Rowsell

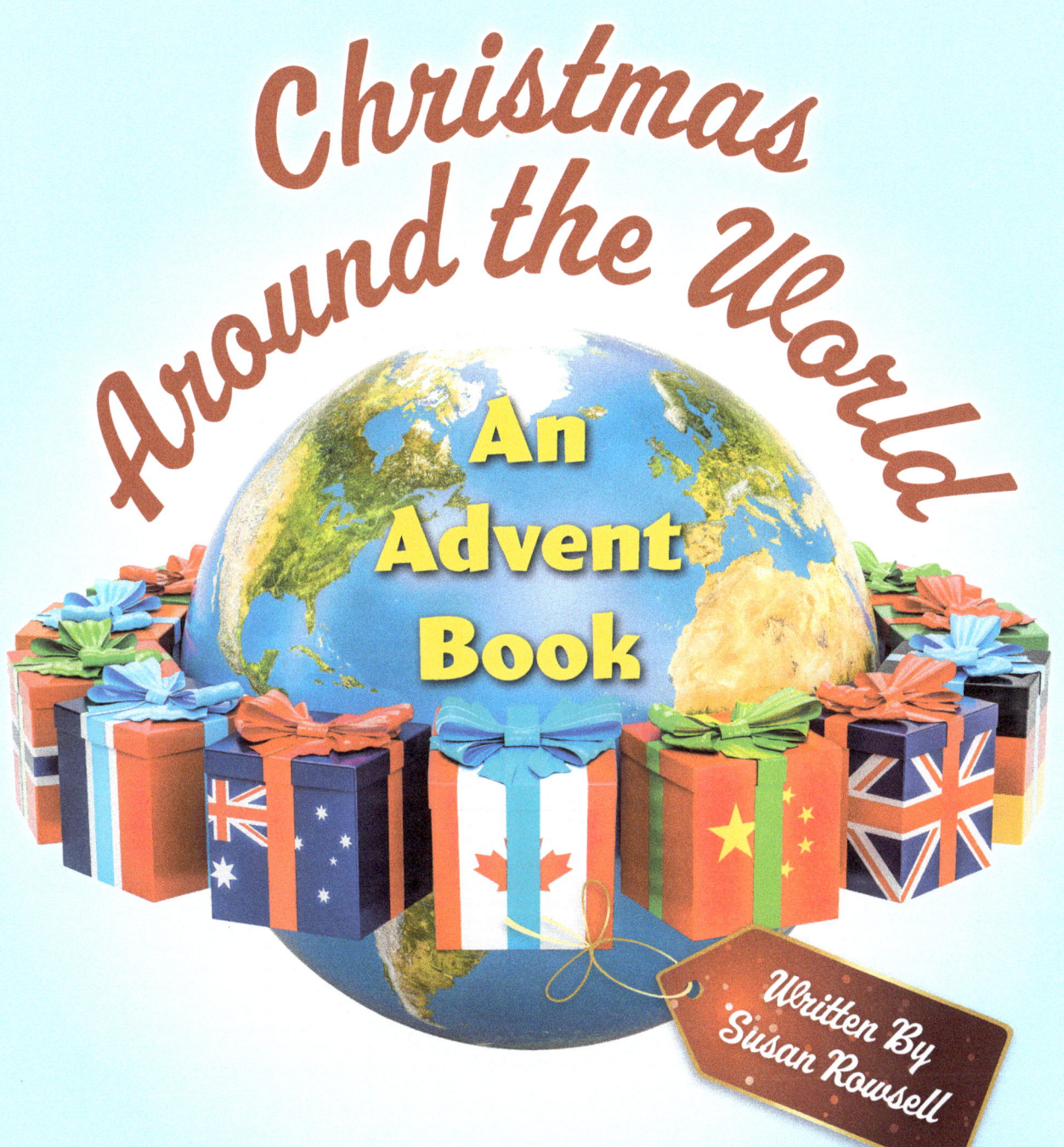

Christmas Around the World

An Advent Book

Written By
Susan Rowsell

 FriesenPress

Suite 300 - 990 Fort St
Victoria, BC, V8V 3K2
Canada

www.friesenpress.com

ISBN
978-1-5255-8193-9 (Hardcover)
978-1-5255-8194-6 (Paperback)
978-1-5255-8195-3 (eBook)

1. *JUVENILE NONFICTION, HOLIDAYS & CELEBRATIONS, CHRISTMAS & ADVENT*

Distributed to the trade by The Ingram Book Company

Dedication

This book is dedicated to my mom, Patsy Alberta Rowsell. My love for Christmas, the magic of the holiday season, the spirit of wonder and goodwill that embraces me each December was a gift I shared with my mom year after year. Her presence is missed all through the year, but I especially miss her as the holiday season unfolds.

I still tear up when our favourite Christmas songs come on. I miss our annual shopping trip and I greatly miss her laughter on Family Christmas Game Night. My mom was often more excited for Santa's arrival than my own children.

For my mom, sister and I, Christmas was always the most wonderful time of the year. This book incorporates my love for Christmas; a gift passed onto me, a gift I will treasure always. A lifetime of memories, traditions, laughter and joy, that I will continue to pass onto my own children. I love you mom, to the moon and back. Merry Merry Christmas.

Pope Julius chose December 25th as the birth of Christ to honour the traditions of the Holiday of Saturnalia. The birth of Christ was first celebrated as the Feast of Nativity. The celebrations spread to Egypt by 432. The Feast of Nativity was celebrated in England by the end of the sixth century. By the end of the eighth century, Christmas was celebrated in Scandinavia.

Christianity began to take over the former Pagan religion. Churches embraced the celebration of Christmas. Christmas became a time when upper class societies shared their wealth with those less fortunate. From the very first Christmas celebrations, it was important that everyone was included in the celebrations. Unity was an essential root of the holiday celebrations, and still is today.

It wasn't until the nineteenth century that Americans began to embrace Christmas. Americans celebrated Christmas differently than the Europeans and other cultures. Christmas wasn't celebrated in an extravagant party styled manner. Christmas was celebrated in a more peaceful and serene way; centring on time spent with family and loved ones.

Christmas rapidly began to evolve around the globe. The celebration of Christmas continues to grow to this day. Even in countries, like China, that don't practise Christianity, people in small regions of the country are beginning to celebrate Christmas. In small regions of India, people are beginning to embrace the celebration of Christmas.

The magical wonder of a North American Christmas sends a yearning to people all around the world. In many European countries, a lot of the ancient traditions and customs are fading away and being replaced by North American traditions. As someone that loves a good old-fashioned North American Christmas, I am also intrigued by many of the traditions from other countries. Over the past few years, I have incorporated some of these traditions into my own holiday festivities.

From my family to yours, I wish you a joyous and magical Christmas season. . . .

The Ten Symbols of Christmas

From Hanukkah and Kwanzaa to Easter and Christmas, all holiday celebrations incorporate symbolism. There are ten main symbols associated with Christmas. They are the star, lights, candles, trees, poinsettias, holly, wreaths, bells, candy canes, stockings, and gifts. Countries all over the world incorporate these symbols into their holiday celebrations.

The star is one of the most recognizable symbols of the Christmas season. The star that sits upon the Christmas tree represents the star that appeared in the sky the night that Jesus Christ was born. This star led the Three Wise Men to the baby Jesus. The Christmas star reminds us to follow the light of Christ and to share that light with others.

One of the most prominent Christmas decorations of all are candles and lights. All over the world, Christmas is a spectacular show of twinkling lights, burning candles, glowing lanterns, and flickering fairy lights. Cities and towns all across the world are aglow as families celebrate the holiday season.

For centuries, candles have brought warmth and brightness to families during the winter months. Candles were used to represent the star that appeared for all to see when the Saviour was born. Candles represent that Jesus Christ is the light of the world. The lights of Christmas remind us to be a light to others.

Even before the birth of Christ, trees that stayed green all year held a special meaning. A green tree in the winter reminded people of hope and new life. The evergreen tree that majestically glows in living rooms around the world is a sign of rebirth and hope in the coming year.

The poinsettia is a plant that thrives in the winter months. The poinsettia is star shaped representing the Christmas star. Red poinsettias resemble the blood of Christ, and white poinsettias resemble the purity of Christ.

Holly is used as a Christmas decoration all over the world because it is a plant that lives all year long. The sharp leaves of the holly leaf resemble the crown of thorns that Christ wore. The red berries symbolize the blood he shed for us. In Scandinavian, the word "holly" translates to mean "Christ thorn."

For centuries, bells have announced Christmas Day as the birth of Christ. When Christ was born, the angels rejoiced and declared, "Glory to God in the highest, and on Earth peace and goodwill towards men."

The candy cane is also known as the candy crook. The shepherds carried their staffs when visiting the baby Jesus. In ancient times, shepherds used their staff to gently lead their sheep to food and water and to lead them away from danger. The candy cane reminds us that Christ will lead us to safety and peace.

Traditionally wreaths are made from greenery and holly. The circular shape of the wreath represents eternity. The hanging of the wreath in one's home is an invitation to others to share in the joy of Christmas.

It may seem odd that the tradition of hanging stockings by the fireplace originated from ancient times when people hung their socks by the fireplace. Like many Christmas symbols, the stocking derives from an old legend. A poor man had three daughters of marrying age, and he didn't have the money for a dowry. In ancient times, it was required that a bride give her husband to be a gift of money upon their marriage. It was very difficult for a woman to get married without a dowry. St. Nicholas offered this father the money he required for his daughters to marry. He was a proud man, and he would not accept his charity. St. Nicholas decided to help the family anonymously. One evening, St. Nicholas threw three bags of gold through the front window of the family's home. The money landed in three socks that were hanging by the fireplace to dry. All three women were able to marry. As you hang your stockings by the fireplace on Christmas Eve, remember they represent the spirit of giving, the spirit of Christmas.

Christmas is the season to give. In countries all over the world, people exchange gifts during the holiday season. People buy gifts for families in need. Families donate gifts of money, food, and toys to charitable foundations. People give the gifts of comfort and joy by inviting people into their homes for meals and holiday cheer. Santa Claus gives gifts to children all over the world, bringing them joy and cheer.

When Christ was born the Three Wise Men brought the newborn baby gifts of gold, frankincense, and myrrh. God gave the gift of his only begotten son.

Remember to give the gifts of compassion, joy, and kindness to others during the holiday season.

Christmas in Canada

Merry Christmas ~ Joyous Noël

The first Christmas celebrated in Canada was in 1535. It was celebrated in a tiny village in Quebec by a small group of people. It had been a cold, bitter winter, and war had brought a lot of death and hardship to the people. And so began the tradition that links the celebration of Christmas all over the world: People gathered together to celebrate with food, song, and cheer.

The first Christmas tree in Canada was displayed in Sorel, Quebec. Germany was the first country to display Christmas trees in their homes during the holiday season. As more and more German descendants moved to Canada, Christmas trees became more popular.

In the nineteenth century, the celebration of Christmas was quickly spreading from province to province.

In Newfoundland, families would bring in a huge Yule log. They would burn the Yule log for the twelve days before Christmas. The people of Newfoundland believed that by burning the Yule log, they would protect their homes from fire in the coming year. In Quebec, children would hang stockings for the Christmas Child to fill with sweets and treats. In Ontario, people went door to door singing Christmas carols. They exchanged beautiful homemade Christmas cards. Homes were open to neighbours; banquet tables were laden with rich foods like roast beef, a boar's head, and plum pudding.

In the prairie provinces, Christmas dinner was more elaborate than the European Christmas dinners. After dinner, people in villages all over the prairie provinces went ice skating. In British Columbia, loggers would go into the mountains weeks before Christmas to cut down Douglas fir trees. Just before Christmas, the loggers would return from the mountains with trees for people to take home and decorate.

Canada is a country diverse in culture, religion, and tradition; and Christmas is celebrated with great grandeur and anticipation. As one of the largest festivals in the world, Christmas in Canada is celebrated in its own unique manner, with influences and cultural variations from all over the world.

For many people in Canada, the celebration of the Christmas season begins in early November, with stores and town streets already aglow in festive colours. The Santa Claus parade in early November marks the beginning of the holiday season in many regions of Canada. The Santa Claus parade in Toronto, Ontario, is one of the oldest and largest Christmas parades in the world. The Toronto Santa Claus parade made its debut in 1913.

Nova Scotia is known worldwide for their Douglas fir trees. Every December, the biggest Douglas fir tree is sent to Boston in the United States. This is how the people of Nova Scotia continue to send their gratitude to Bostonians for their help after the Halifax

Explosion. In Quebec, they celebrate *La Fête des Rois*, on January 6th. A cake is baked and placed in the centre of the table with a bean inside. Whichever family member or guest seated at the table gets the piece of cake with the bean inside gets to play king or queen for the day. Labrador City in Newfoundland hosts Christmas light and ice sculpture contests.

In northern Canada, there are taffy parties. These parties are held in honour of St. Catherine, the patron saint of single women. These festive parties introduce single men and women. As in the prairie provinces, ice skating is a popular tradition in Quebec. After skating families enjoy homemade holiday cookies and hot chocolate and eggnog.

The children of Canada believe in Santa Claus: a jolly, plump old man dressed in red and white, who carries a red sack full of presents in a sleigh driven by magical flying reindeer.

The true countdown to Christmas begins on December 1st. Advent calendars filled with little chocolates or gifts help children countdown the days until Santa Claus arrives. Many children also enjoy a different Christmas story during the nights of Advent.

There are parades and festivities. Christmas cards are mailed to family and friends. Letters are sent to Santa Claus at the North Pole. Canadians enjoy Christmas carols and Christmas music. Many Canadian families enjoy watching Christmas movies, classics like *National Lampoon's Christmas Vacation, Elf,* and *It's a Wonderful Life.* The shopping centres are decorated and filled with the hustle and bustle of holiday shoppers. Families enjoy the season together baking cookies, tobogganing, ice skating, making crafts, watching holiday movies, shopping, wrapping, and hosting holiday parties.

On Christmas Eve, stockings are hung by the fireplace. The tree lights twinkle as many families settle in for a cosy, silent night. Cookies and milk are put out for Santa and carrots for his reindeer. Some children even leave bird seed and nuts outside for all the forest animals. Stories are read and children snuggle into bed dreaming of flying reindeer.

On Christmas morning, gifts are exchanged. Families all across Canada enjoy a festive feast with family and loved ones. Festive meals vary from province to province, from turkey and the trimmings to fresh caught lobster. Christmas Day is a peaceful and serene time for families, as the hustle and bustle of the holiday season comes to an end.

Merry Christmas from our great country to yours as we celebrate Christmas around the world.

The Christmas Tree

Long before Christmas was celebrated, plants and trees that stayed green all year long held a special meaning for people in the winter. Just as people today celebrate Christmas with evergreen trees and wreaths, ancient people hung evergreen boughs over their doors and windows. They believed evergreens kept witches, ghosts, evil spirits, and illness away.

In the northern hemisphere, the shortest day of the year is December 21st, the first day of winter. Many ancient people believed the sun was a god, and winter came because the Sun God was sick. They hung evergreens in their homes to remind them of the sunny green days that would return when the Sun God was well again.

Germany was the first country to decorate Christmas trees during the holiday season. Martin Luther, a sixteenth-century pastor, was walking home one evening writing a sermon. He was bedazzled by the light of the stars shining on the snow laden evergreen trees. To recapture the scene for his family, he put an evergreen tree in his living room and wired its branches with lighted candles.

In 1846, Queen Victoria and Prince Albert published a family portrait sitting around a Christmas tree. The Christmas tree immediately became popular across England.

By the 1890s, Christmas ornaments were shipped from Germany to countries all over the world. Christmas tree popularity was quickly growing in the United States. While the Europeans preferred smaller trees, the Americans liked their Christmas trees tall and wide. Christmas trees began appearing in town squares and were becoming a worldwide holiday tradition. The Rockefeller Christmas tree in New York City dates back to the depression era. In 1948, a 100-foot Norway spruce stood tall at the Rockefeller Center. Today, the famous Rockefeller Christmas Tree is laden with over 25,000 lights!

German and Italian settlers arrived in Canada in the 1700s. They brought gingerbread houses, Advent calendars, Christmas cookies, and the Christmas tree.

In Norway, families take a trip into the woods and cut down their Christmas tree. The children play in their bedrooms while their parents decorate the tree. Families then join hands and sing and dance around the Christmas tree.

The tallest living Christmas tree was a 120-foot ninety-one-year-old Douglas fir in Woodinville, Washington.

From continent to continent, Christmas is celebrated with many different traditions and customs. In countries, homes nationwide celebrate the holiday season with the ever-popular Christmas tree. Each season, Christmas trees are decorated with love, adorned with memories of seasons passed.

Susan Rowsell

December 3rd

Christmas in the United States of America

Merry Christmas

The United States of America was one of the very last countries to celebrate Christmas due to religious indifferences. In the seventeenth century, the Puritans came into power, and in 1645, they cancelled the celebrations of Christmas. Shortly after Christmas was banned, a new king came into power and reinstated the celebration of Christmas. However, due to the high number of Puritans living in the United States at the time, Christmas was still prohibited in certain states. In 1650, anyone in Boston who tried to celebrate Christmas or portrayed the Christmas spirit in any way was fined five shillings.

On December 25th, 1789, the American Revolution Congress held a meeting and voted to declare the first official celebration of Christmas. On June 26th, 1870, Christmas was declared a national holiday in the United States. There were still a lot of conflicting views on the celebration of Christmas throughout the country.

Northern Americans chose not to celebrate Christmas. They celebrated Thanksgiving with great grandeur. Southern Americans embraced the social aspects of Christmas and celebrated both Christmas and Thanksgiving.

After the civil war ended, Americans worked together to encourage the celebration of Christmas. After a long hard war, Americans bonded together to embrace the magic of the holiday season and build a united nation.

Authors began illustrating books displaying the wonders of a North American Christmas. Picture books of Santa Claus began to circulate. Churches encouraged the celebration of Christmas as the birth of Christ. Women's magazines illustrated recipes, crafts, and decorating tips for the holiday season.

By the end of the nineteenth century, Americans were embracing the holiday season with great flair and great cheer.

In 1931, Coca-Cola launched the plump, jolly old Santa Claus that is captured in Christmas displays and advertisements all across North America. In 1924, the first Macy's Day Thanksgiving Day Parade debuted. The Macy's Thanksgiving Day Parade is the launch of the holiday season in New York City. The tree lighting ceremony at Rockefeller Center is an eighty-year-old tradition in New York City. This ceremony takes place one week after Thanksgiving. A seventy to ninety-foot Norway spruce is illuminated on Rockefeller Plaza.

The first Rockefeller Christmas Tree was a small twenty-foot balsam fir tree. This tree made its debut in 1931, during the Great Depression. It was decorated by construction workers who had been working on the construction of the Rockefeller Plaza. They decorated the tree with cranberries, garlands of paper, and some tin cans. The tallest Christmas tree at the Rockefeller Center was a one-hundred-foot spruce in 1999. In 2007, the Rockefeller tree was donated to Habitat for Humanity, a charitable organization that builds homes for families in need.

From state to state, Americans have unique Christmas traditions.

The Moravians in Pennsylvania make a small village under the Christmas tree called "putz." This was a common tradition in the early colonial American Moravian communities. These nativity scenes could become very elaborate, often including saw dust to represent roads leading to the manger. There were often carved wooden people representing the holy people. By the nineteenth century, the putz could be seen displayed on mantles and around fireplaces.

In Alaska, people decorated the entrance to their homes with a pineapple. This is a sign of friendliness to people as they enter their homes.

In Washington, an enormous Christmas tree is lit by the president. In Boston, they love to sing Christmas carols. In Arizona, *Las Posadas* is a famous Mexican ritual that is celebrated. Families visit one another's homes in search of Mary and Joseph.

In the South, Louisiana families in small communities along the Mississippi River light bonfires along the river banks to help guide Santa's way.

The countdown to Christmas begins on December 1st. Children eagerly countdown the days until Santa's arrival on the 24th of December. December is a month full of family get-togethers, office Christmas parties, and school Christmas plays. American families like to string popcorn to decorate their Christmas trees, and they love decorating gingerbread houses.

Christmas Eve is a family night. Festive meals usually consist of turkey and ham with vegetables and lots of stuffing and gravies. The Americans enjoy a rich assortment of desserts, from pies and cakes to cookies and tarts. Stockings are hung by the chimney in hopes that Santa Claus will fill them with treats while the children are sleeping. Gifts are exchanged on Christmas morning. The Christmas festivities continue through to New Year's Day.

Christmas in New York City

Merry Christmas

New York City is famous worldwide for some of the most extravagant holiday celebrations during the Christmas season. The Macy's Day Thanksgiving Day Parade has been marking the beginning of the holiday season in New York since 1924. During the 1920s, the parade was staged by employee's from Macy's department store. Many of these employees immigrated from Europe. They loved participating in the parade preparations, as it reminded them of the grand celebrations from their homeland. In 1927, the gigantic balloons, which are the signature element of the parade, made their debut. Today, the Macy's Day Parade consists of more than twenty-five floats, more than ten marching bands, and several large character balloons.

New Yorkers enjoy walking the city streets gazing at all the beautiful Christmas lights and displays while sipping hot chocolate. Families enjoy ice skating at the Rockefeller Center and attending the Holiday Train show at the Botanical Gardens.

The Rockefeller Tree Lighting Ceremony takes place in early December. The ceremony now includes live entertainment, dancing, and *hor d'oeuvres*. Families can also enjoy a full course dinner. Families can purchase a keepsake ornament for their Christmas tree.

Many New Yorkers enjoy making their own Advent calendars. One style of calendar is made with a clue in each window that leads to a hidden treat. Another style of calendar designates a family member to put an ornament on the Christmas tree for each of the twenty-four days of Christmas, ending with the star.

Many people in New York also enjoy participating in the famous cookie crawl. This is a festive game that local bakeries participate in. A scavenger hunt is designed for participants who get to enjoy various holiday baked goods from local bakeries. There is also a hot chocolate crawl.

People in New York enjoy making homemade Christmas cards, singing Christmas carols, sleigh rides, snowball fights, and ice sculpture and snowman building contests.

New York City can take on a magical glow during the holiday season when the city is covered in a blanket of white. The laughter of children frolicking in the snow, sleigh rides and evening strolls, fresh baked cookies and hot cocoa—New York is a magical winter wonderland to savour and enjoy.

Susan Rowsell

Christmas in Hawaii

Mele Kalikimaka

Hawaiian residents begin putting up their holiday lights as soon as the last bit of Thanksgiving turkey is gobbled up. December in Hawaii is full of joyous concerts, community parades, and dazzling displays of holiday cheer throughout the islands.

Christmas was introduced to Hawaii in 1820 when Protestant missionaries came to Hawaii from New England. Celebrating Christmas in Hawaii was intertwined with an ancient celebration called "*Makahiki*." This celebration lasted for four months with great feasts and games. War and conflict were strictly forbidden during these festivities.

In 1856, Alexander Liholiho declared December 25th to be his kingdom's national holiday of Thanksgiving. Santa Claus made his first appearance to Hawaii in 1858, arriving by boat on Waikiki Beach. He left gifts for all the children of Hawaii at Washington Palace where the governor resides.

Poinsettias are very popular in Hawaii. Wreaths are made from local plants and displayed around the islands.

Honolulu Lights is a festive holiday spectacular in Hawaii. It is held at the Honolulu City Hall in early December. A fifty-foot Norfolk pine tree is set aglow. There is a festival that follows with Christmas tree and wreath exhibits, giant Yuletide displays, and live entertainment.

The Christmas Luau is a festive feast consisting of roasted pig, salmon, and other food delicacies. *Haupia* is a traditional coconut milk-based dessert.

There is no kissing under the mistletoe in Hawaii; embraces take place under the palm trees.

From the sandy beaches of Hawaii to the snow-covered mountains of Colorado, Americans celebrate with different traditions and customs. From state to state and home to home, the celebrations of Christmas may vary, but the message remains the same, Christmas in the United States of America is a time for unity and peace. May your holiday celebrations bring you unity and peace with unified greetings of cheer from the United States of America.

December **4th**

Christmas in Britain

Merry Christmas

The origins of the Christmas celebrations in Britain date back to 596 AD when St. Augustine brought Christianity to the country. The Christmas season in Great Britain begins in early November and carries through until January 6th.

During the Christmas season, families make holiday wreaths consisting of three pink, one white, and one purple candle to symbolize the Christmas Advent. Christmas trees can be seen in stores, markets, town squares, churches, and homes all over the country. Homes are also decorated with holly, ivy, mistletoe, and poinsettias. Poinsettias are exchanged as gifts throughout the Christmas season.

Children write letters to Father Christmas in early December. They throw their letters in the fireplace. It is believed their letters will float to the North Pole.

Susan Rowsell

Many churches throughout Britain host a special service on the fourth day of Advent called the Christingle Service. This service is based on a Christmas carol dating back to Scandinavian times. During this ceremony, a child receives an orange wrapped in a red ribbon, signifying the blood of Christ.

Christmas Eve is an exciting night for children as they anticipate the arrival of Father Christmas. Children leave him a piece of mince pie and a glass of sherry or milk. They hang their stockings by the fireplace before attending evening church services.

In Britain, children don't get to open their presents on Christmas morning. They have to wait until after dinner. Christmas dinner is served in the late afternoon. The British enjoy roasted turkey with all the trimmings. Plum pudding is served with hidden treasures inside that symbolize good luck for the coming year. Everyone pops Christmas crackers and wears a paper crown, a very traditional custom in Britain. Families listen to the Queen's speech, which is aired during dinner. Minced pies and fruity puddings are served for dessert. And finally, the moment of anticipation has arrived, families open their presents from Father Christmas. After presents are opened families enjoy a relaxing evening of playing board games and singing Christmas carols.

On Boxing Day, families enjoy a more relaxing day with more festive food. Some families enjoy the day at the local pub.

In Britain the festivities end on January 6th, Three Kings' Day. The British conclude the Christmas festivities with great holiday flair. Large parties are thrown in regions all across the country. Folks enjoy great food, desserts, and lots of beer. There is a lot of singing and dancing. Dinner is served in the early afternoon. It is traditional in Great Britain to burn the Yule log throughout the twelve days of Christmas to ensure good luck for the coming year. During the twelve days of Christmas, the British eat a lot of mince pie; it is said that you will receive one month of good luck for every mince pie you eat. The Christmas festivities come to an end in Britain with a jolly toast for the new year—wishing good will and prosperity to family and friends.

Warm wishes and good cheer to you and yours, from Britain!

Christmas in Scotland

Merry Christmas ~ Nollaig Chridheil

The celebration of Christmas was banned in Scotland for over four hundred years. It wasn't until 1958 that December 25th was declared a national holiday in Scotland.

Today in Scotland, the celebrations of the holiday season begin just days before Halloween. Stores begin selling decorations, craft supplies, baking goods, and other seasonal items. Department stores and buildings are dressed in holiday lights. Multi-coloured light bulbs are placed in big fir trees in some of the smaller towns across Scotland. In the days leading to Christmas, young people smash the lights one by one to countdown the days until Christmas.

Children make their own Advent calendars. These pretty craft calendars have little doors revealing a festive picture for the twenty-four days of Christmas. In early December, children write their letters to Santa Claus and place them in the fireplace where they magically make their way to the North Pole.

Throughout December, homes are decorated with trees, coloured lights, tinsel, poinsettias, and other pretty seasonal flowers.

In many regions of Scotland, Christmas Eve is called *"Sowans Nicht."* This name symbolizes a traditional dish eaten on Christmas Eve in many homes across the country. It is a dish made from oat husks. A popular Christmas tradition in Scotland is burning the branches from a rowan tree. This signifies that any bad feelings between family and friends will be forgotten over the Yuletide season. In homes all across Scotland, a fire burns all through the night. The Scottish believe that if the fire goes out, they will suffer bad luck in the coming year. In many Scottish homes, families enjoy an open-air lunch on Christmas Eve. Families enjoy roasted duck, smoked salmon, mince pies, plum pudding, black buns, cakes made from fruit, and several Yule log desserts.

On Christmas Eve, children hang their stockings or pillowcases by the fire to be filled by Santa Claus. In some homes, children leave out a treat of cookies and milk. In other homes, children leave Santa a piece of mince pie and a glass of sherry. Many children leave carrots for the reindeer. A candle stays lit in the window, welcoming strangers inside to share in the festive activities. This is a tribute to the Holy Family, who struggled to find shelter on the eve of Christ's birth.

The Scottish celebrate the coming year with great grandeur and zest. There are parades, concerts, parties, large bonfires, firework displays, and lots of singing, dancing, eating, and drinking. Some families burn juniper branches in their homes. They open the windows to release the smoke and evil spirits.

The first visitor to enter a person's home on New Year's Day is called the "first footer." This person must give gifts of peat, money, and bread. These gifts symbolize warmth, wealth, and lack of want. The Scottish celebrate the new year with great enthusiasm and zest, hoping to bring good luck to their homes and families in the coming year.

Blessings of love, joy, and peace, from Scotland.

Susan Rowsell

History of the Christmas Cracker

Christmas crackers have been a traditional part of the holiday season since Victorian times. The British claim the Christmas cracker was introduced by a British man by the name of Tom Smith in the mid 1840s. While Tom was visiting France, he was intrigued by the French holiday treat, known as the *bonbon*. The bonbon was a sugary almond treat wrapped in coloured paper.

After some time had passed, Tom marketed his own version of the bonbon. Sales were great during the holiday season, but Tom felt his invention still needed some work. One evening while Tom was sitting by his fire, the crackle from the log burning gave him the idea that the bonbon needed to make a crackle sound. Tom incorporated a friction activated explosion from silver fulminate inside the bonbon. He made them a little larger. Originally, Tom named his new invention the *cosaque*. Eventually, they became known as the Christmas cracker.

Christmas crackers held small toys, puzzles, paper crowns, and very lame jokes. In fact, Christmas crackers became traditionally popular for their paper crowns and jokes. The paper crowns symbolized the crowns worn during the ancient Saturnalia celebrations. It is a British tradition to have Christmas crackers displayed on the dinner table during the Christmas meal. After dinner, families enjoy sharing their jokes around the table.

Susan Rowsell

How did Scrooge win the football game?

The ghost of Christmas passed.

What did Adam say to his wife the day before Christmas?

It's Christmas, Eve.

What is Santa's favourite type of music?

Wrap.

The largest Christmas cracker on record measured 207 feet long by thirteen feet wide. This cracker was made by the parents of preschool children in Buckinghamshire, England, on December 20th, 2001. This cracker was filled with balloons, toys, paper crowns, and jokes.

The largest pull of a Christmas cracker was in Japan at the Honda Festival on October 18th, 2009. This cracker was pulled by 1,478 people.

December 5th

Christmas in Australia

Merry Christmas

Christmas in Australia is celebrated with sunny blue skies and intense heat. Children are on summer vacation from school, and many families take vacation time during the holiday season. Australia is the world's largest island and the world's smallest continent. Many of Australia's immigrants came from England and Ireland and brought their Christmas traditions with them.

The Christmas season in Australia begins in late November. Children partake in Christmas plays and concerts. They write letters to Santa Clause. Homes, stores, and town squares take on a festive glow with brightly coloured lights, tinsel, and bells. Christmas trees are decorated with images of Australian wildlife and landmarks. Cotton balls are often used as a decoration to represent snow. Small statues of native animals wearing Santa hats pulled by kangaroos are often displayed in town squares.

Christmas bells, the Christmas bush, Christmas trees, palm trees, and the Christmas orchard are all native plants that grow during the holiday season in Australia.

Carols by Candlelight is a festive outdoor concert held during the holiday season. Christmas carols are sung by candlelight as families bond together on a magical December night.

On Christmas Eve, Australians with an Irish background light a large candle in the front window of their homes. The candle is lit by the youngest child in the family. The candle glows throughout the night to welcome Mary and Joseph into the warm comforts of their home.

Some families enjoy a warm festive meal of roast meats, vegetables, fruit cakes, and puddings. Puddings are made with a gold nugget inside. The family member or guest that receives the gold nugget will be blessed with good fortune in the coming year. Other families enjoy barbecues on the beach or picnic dinners at the park, with cold meats, seafood, and soft meringue cakes with whipped cream and fruit.

Santa Claus visits on Christmas Eve. Some children believe he is dressed in his red and white fur-trimmed attire, while others believe him to come in his comfortable beach wear. Children leave Santa a piece of cake and a glass of milk or a pint of beer. Santa leaves gifts for the children under the tree and in their stockings.

Families gather on Christmas morning to exchange gifts. Families love to sing Christmas carols around the Christmas tree.

Boxing Day is another fun-filled day for families across Australia. There is the Boxing Day Test match, which is a famous cricket game. The Sydney Harbour Race is also held on Boxing Day. There are a lot of barbecues, picnics, boat rides, and outdoor games.

Australians of British or Irish descent leave tips for their grocers, postal workers, and newspaper carriers as a way of sending their gratitude for the hard work they do all year long.

The Twelfth Night is a festive celebration that occurs on January 6th. This celebration marks the end of the holiday season in Australia.

Happy Holidays, from the land Down Under.

Susan Rowsell

Christmas in New Zealand

Merry Christmas

Like their neighbours, the Australians, the people of New Zealand celebrate Christmas during the carefree days of summer.

Shops, stores, and town squares are decorated with Santa Claus figurines and snow scenes. The *pohutukawa* is the Christmas tree of New Zealand. These trees are said to guard the entrance to the sacred cove, through which spirits pass on their way to the next world. There are competitions all over New Zealand for the most festively decorated homes.

The Coca-Cola Christmas in the Park Celebration is one of the largest Christmas parties in the world. This celebration takes place in early December and represents freedom for the people of New Zealand as they break free from the religious rulings of the Queen. The people of New Zealand are embarking on a more modern approach to the holiday season. Christmas in the park is a musical extravaganza. This event sponsors talented new entertainment, as well as a selection of long-standing Kiwi entertainment. A seventy-foot Christmas tree stands aglow amidst the December night sky.

On Christmas Eve, there are carol services throughout the countries. The birth of Christ is celebrated in churches all throughout the island. The children leave out treats for Santa Claus, from cookies and milk to hot apple pie and a glass of sherry.

On Christmas Eve, families enjoy a traditional meal of roasted turkey, vegetables, rich gravies, and sauces and pastries filled with chopped dried fruit. Other families enjoy barbecued burgers and sausages or fish and chips at the local pub. Pavlova, a delicious meringue pie with whipped cream and fresh fruit, is a festive favourite dessert.

Gifts are opened on Christmas Day. Families relax and enjoy good food and drink. Families enjoy playing soccer and other outdoor games as the holiday celebrations come to an end in New Zealand.

Island greetings, from New Zealand.

Susan Rowsell

December **6th**

Christmas in Germany

Fröhliche Weihnachten

Christmas, or *Weihnachten* in Germany, is the most important holiday celebration of the year. The weeks leading up to Christmas include many traditions and customs of diverse origins. Christmas in Germany begins on the first Sunday of Advent. Homemade Christmas cookies, gingerbread houses, nativity scenes, hand-carved nutcrackers, and Christmas pyramids are just some of the signs that the Christmas season has begun in Germany.

The Advent wreath is adorned with four candles: One candle is lit on each of the four Sundays of Advent. The first Advent wreath, which appeared in the nineteenth century, had four large candles and nineteen small candles to help children countdown the days until Christmas. The children of Germany also use a chocolate Advent calendar to countdown the days of Christmas.

Christmas markets are very popular in Germany. Townspeople gather together and listen to brass music, drink beer, and apple cider while shopping for homemade baked goods and gifts. Vendors sell baked goods, including gingerbread hearts, sugar-roasted almonds and cotton candy. Vendors also sell wooden toys and hand-blown glass ornaments. Christmas markets date back to the fourteenth century. At one time, Christmas markets were the only place where people could purchase holiday merchandise.

The Christkindlmarket is one of the oldest and most popular markets in Germany. It is over 365 years old. There are over two hundred vendors. This market is known for their gold foil angels and locally baked gingerbread cakes.

St. Nicholas Day is celebrated on December 6th and in many European countries. Children leave their shoes by the door in hopes that St. Nicholas will fill them with nuts and sweets. Naughty children will find their shoes filled with coal.

In Germany, Christmas is celebrated on Christmas Eve, the holy night. In Germany, the Christmas tree is called the "*tannenbaum.*" Some families decorate their trees on Christmas Eve, while other families decorate their trees at the beginning of Advent. Trees are decorated with tinsel, glass balls, and sweets. A star or an angel sits atop the tree. Many German Christmas trees are decorated with lighted candles instead of electrical lights.

There is a large Christmas tree displayed in front of Windsor Palace. It was a gift from the Germans to the Queen of England. All the glass ornaments displayed on the tree were made in Germany. Well into the twentieth century, Germans would hang their Christmas trees from the ceiling so they would take up less space.

The first known Christmas tree in Germany was set up in 1419 by town bakers, who decorated the tree with fruit, nuts, and baked goods. The town's children got to eat all the treats on New Year's Day. Since the Middle Ages, Germans have decorated their homes with mistletoe, holly, and evergreen boughs during the winter months. In northern Germany, where forests were sparse at this time, they made Christmas pyramids because there weren't enough trees to cut down. They made a pyramid using sticks that were decorated with fir branches.

During the Christmas season, thousands of Germans across the country gather at soccer stadiums and sing Christmas carols by candlelight.

In Germany, Santa Claus is known as *Weihnachtsmann.* He arrives on Christmas Eve. He doesn't descend down the chimney while children are sleeping; he sneaks into homes while children are playing in their rooms. When he has finished filling stockings and placing presents under the tree, he rings a bell to let children know he has come and gone. Families enjoy a festive feast and attend Midnight Mass.

The Christmas Day feast in Germany is quite elaborate and consists of goose, apple and sausage stuffing, red cabbage, and potato dumplings. Cinnamon star cookies are a favourite festive dessert.

The Christmas festivities come to an end on January 6th, which is known as Three King's Day. Children dress up as the Three Wise Men and go door to door singing Christmas carols and blessing homes with good fortune for the coming year. Children also collect money for charitable foundations.

Holiday wishes and good luck greetings, from Germany.

Susan Rowsell

Christmas in Hungary

Boldog Karácsonyt

In Hungary, the Christmas season begins on the first day of Advent. The period of Advent in Hungary is used to decorate and prepare for Christmas. Advent wreaths are hung in schools, offices, shops, and homes. Candles decorated with red and green ribbons can be found in homes across the country. Red and gold are the most commonly used colours for decorating in Hungary; these colours are said to be prosperous.

Families bake biscuits and cookies together for the Christmas banquet, held on Christmas Day. It is customary in Hungary for the Christmas tree to be decorated on Christmas Eve. In some homes, the Christmas tree is decorated by angels as a gift to families.

In Hungary, Santa Claus is called "*Mikulás.*" He visits children on St. Nicholas Day. Children leave their boots on the windowsill. Good boys and girls will awake in the morning to find their boots filled with chocolates, tangerines, apples, dates, candies, and walnuts. Naughty children will find devil figurines in their boots. St. Nicholas Day is celebrated in schools, colleges, and hospitals all around the country. Children all get the opportunity to sit on his lap and sing a Christmas carol with him. St. Nicholas also loves to read the children stories and hand out presents.

Christmas in Hungary is a very religious holiday. An ancient tradition in Hungary that is still practised in some regions of the country is the reacting of the Christmas story. Boys dress up in costumes and go door to door with models of the Holy Family. They sing and dance and act out plays.

St. Luca Day is celebrated in regions of Hungary on December 13th. All of the men begin carving a wooden stool, known as the Luca stool. The Luca stool must be complete by Christmas Eve. The men bring their stools to Midnight Mass and stand on them scanning the church for witches. After identifying the witches, they run home. They drop poppy seeds along the way to distract the witches. If they do not get home before the witches and throw their stools in the fire, they will be harmed.

Christmas Eve is the most important night of the holiday celebrations in Hungary. Christmas Eve is called *"Szenteste."* Families spend time together singing Christmas carols around the tree. Children write letters to Baby Jesus on Christmas Eve, asking for special toys and gifts. Parents will ring a bell when it is time for presents to be opened. Families enjoy a festive feast together. Tables are decorated with green fir twigs. Oranges and polished red apples are used for the table setting. This setting symbolizes peasant culture, health, and love. It is traditional in many Hungarian homes to eat fish during Advent. Many families enjoy a fish soup, along with turkey with chestnut stuffing and a bountiful of desserts with poppy seeds. Poppy seeds are considered to be a fertility charm during the harvest season. The Hungarians also enjoy wine during the evening.

The Christmas festivities in Hungary conclude with the new year's celebrations. Families gather to give thanks for the year that has passed and give gratitude for the year to come.

Holiday blessings, from Hungary.

Susan Rowsell

History of the Advent Calendar

Advent began as a four-week period of time beginning on the Sunday nearest to the Feast of St. Andrew, the apostle, on November 30th. Advent ended on December 25th, the birth of Christ. Many Advent calendars today commence on December 1st and continue to December 25th.

The traditions of the Advent calendar date back to the nineteenth century when German Protestants made chalk marks on doors or lit candles to countdown the days until Christmas. Many Germans still partake in this ancient tradition.

In 1904, Gerhard Lang included an Advent calendar in a local German newspaper. His calendar featured twenty-four coloured pictures attached to a piece of cardboard. His idea was inspired by his mother, who made such calendars for him when he was a boy. She would call them "The Christmas Calendar." He later modified his calendar to include little doors. During World War II, there was a shortage of cardboard and the production of the Advent calendar stopped. Shortly after the war ended, Richard Sellmer resumed the production of the Advent calendar and its popularity began to soar.

Another company produced Advent calendars with Bible verses behind each door.

President Dwight Eisenhower popularized Advent calendars in the United States after he was photographed opening one with his grandchildren. Production of Advent calendars with chocolates behind the doors began in 1958.

One of the most expensive Advent calendars to hit the market was a four-foot Christmas shaped structure carved from elm and walnut wood. Each of the twenty-four doors contained a piece of organic chocolate. These calendars sold for $50,000 a piece, with the proceeds supporting cocoa farmers in Belize.

One year in Gloucester, England, a building in King's Square was transformed into the largest known Advent calendar. This interactive calendar was designed to promote local businesses during the holiday season. Each day of December, a door was opened to reveal a special deal at a local business.

Toy companies have gotten into the marketing of the Advent calendar as well. You can find Advent calendars featuring Lego, Crayola, and many others.

Counting down the days until Christmas is a long-standing tradition that has continued to grow in popularity among both children and adults alike.

Christmas in Russia

S Rozhdestvom

Christmas in Russia is celebrated differently than in many other countries. The people of Russia believe in Jesus Christ and his mother Mary. The old Julian calendar dates Christmas on the 7th of January; and this is when Russians celebrate Christmas.

At one time the legend of St. Nicholas was very vital to the Russian culture. In the seventeenth century, Prince Vladmir travelled to Constantinople to be baptised. He returned home and shared many enlightening stories about St. Nicholas of Myra and his generosity and magical healing powers. The Feast of St. Nicholas was celebrated on December 6th for many centuries. After the Russian Revolution, the feast was cancelled. St. Nicholas was replaced by Grandfather Frost.

Before 1917, Christmas in Russia was celebrated in a similar manner to many other

Susan Rowsell

countries. After 1917, all of the Christmas celebrations were incorporated into the celebrations of the new year. In Russia, Christmas officially begins on December 31st and ends on January 10th. For many Russians, Christmas is known as the Winter Festival. In some regions of Russia, Russians continue to celebrate Christmas in a more traditional manner.

Russians like to decorate their gardens with lights and Christmas ornaments. Christmas trees are called "*yolka.*" Christmas trees are decorated with ornaments, flowers, and lights.

Christmas Eve in Russia is on January 6th. Russians fast for forty days before Christmas. Christmas Eve begins when the first star appears in the night sky. The family begins dinner by eating *kutya*, which is a porridge made from wheat berries, fruit, nuts, and honey. The family shares the porridge from one bowl. When everyone has had their share, they throw one spoonful at the ceiling. If the porridge sticks to the ceiling, the family will have good luck and a bountiful harvest in the coming year. Christmas Eve dinner commences when the father of the family recites the Lord's prayer. They enjoy a meal of vegetables, soups, salads, and homemade pies. Families love to sing, dance, and drink the night away.

In some regions of Russia, children receive their gifts from Grandfather Frost and his granddaughter, Snow Maiden. In other regions of Russia, children receive their gifts from Baboushka, the elderly woman who got lost on her way to find the baby Jesus.

Christmas Day is celebrated with a grand feast. This festive meal consists of twelve courses, representing the twelve apostles of Christ. Hay is spread across the floor and the table in belief that horse feed will be plentiful in the coming year. During dinner, family members make clucking noises so hens will lay a bountiful of eggs in the coming year. The father of the table commences dinner by declaring that Jesus Christ has been born. The mother of the table applies honey on the foreheads of all the family members and guests at the table so that sweet things will come in the year ahead. A white candle burns brightly at the centre of the table to signify that Jesus Christ is the light of the world. A traditional bread called *pagach* is dipped in honey and garlic and shared around the table to symbolize that Jesus Christ is the bread of life.

After dinner families open presents and then attend Midnight Mass. Families stay up late into the morning hours dancing, singing, and drinking as they celebrate the birth of Jesus Christ.

Peace and joy to you and yours, from Russia.

Christmas in Greece

Kalá Christoúgenna

Christmas in Greece has become more of a celebrated holiday in recent years. Easter has always been the most important holiday celebration in Greece. Christmas in Greece begins on December 6th, with the celebration of St. Nicholas Day, and ends on January 6th, Epiphany Day.

St. Nicholas is a very customary legend in Greece. He is highly regarded as the patron saint of sailors. He wears drenched clothing and brine in his beard. He drips with sea water and sweat as he struggles with the force of the ocean to save ships from sinking. Greek ships never leave port without an icon of St. Nicholas aboard. During the Christmas season, many ships are decorated with festive lights to honour the patron saint of sailors.

During the Christmas season, towns and cities are decorated with festive flair. In big cities throughout Greece, there are huge musical festivals and plays during the holiday season. There are little elf houses that sell candies to children and several festive activities for children to partake in. Christmas carollers travel through the streets spreading Christmas cheer. Evergreen trees are decorated in homes and town squares. Trees are decorated with tinsel and ornaments. A sparkling star sits atop the tree. Some families in

Greece place a pomegranate on the ground and enter their homes with their right foot, intending to bring good luck to the family in the coming year.

The most symbolic decoration in Greece is a shallow wooden bowl with a piece of wire suspended across the rim, from which hangs a sprig of basil wrapped around a wooden cross. Water is kept in the bowl to keep the basil fresh. Every day of the holiday season, the mother of the household dips the cross and the basil into some holy water and sprinkles it around the house. This is done to keep the goblins away. *Kallikántzaroi* are mischievous spirits that cause havoc during the twelve days of Christmas. It is believed that the kali partake in mischievous behaviour because the Christ Child has not yet been baptised. The kali extinguish fires, braid horse's hair, sour the milk, and eat food and sweets that have been prepared for Christmas. Some families keep a fire burning throughout the twelve days of Christmas to prevent the kali from entering their homes through the chimney.

On Christmas Eve, young boys go from home to home singing Christmas carols while beating drums and playing the triangle. They spread Christmas cheer through their music and are given almonds, dry figs, and coins.

After forty days of fasting, the Christmas Eve feast is a grand one, consisting of roast pork or turkey, roast lamb, vegetables, stuffing filled with pine cones, and lots and lots of delicious desserts. *Melomakarona* is a festive cookie made with cinnamon and cloves that is drenched in honey. *Christopsomo* bread is baked with a cross on top to honour the Christ Child.

In Greece, Santa Claus is known as *Agios Vassilis*. He was an ancient saint who was generous and kind to his people. He visits the children of Greece on January 1st. The Greek are simple and quaint in their gift giving. They like to give gifts to local orphanages and charitable organizations. *Vasilopita* cake is eaten on New Year's Day. The cake is baked with a coin inside. The current year is engraved on the top of the cake with almonds. The person who receives the coin in their piece of cake is bestowed good luck for the coming year. Everyone wishes one another *"Hronia Polla,"* which means "Happy New Year."

The Christmas festivities end in grand flair on January 6th. The Greeks bless the waters. A cross is thrown into the water and thousands of brave people jump into the chilly waters to retrieve the cross. The person who retrieves the cross is granted good luck in the coming year.

Many happy years, from the people of Greece.

Christmas in Bethlehem

Merry Christmas

Christmas is not celebrated in many parts of Israel and Palestine, as a most people are Jewish or Muslim. The Jewish people in Israel celebrate Hanukkah. In many parts of these countries, there are no Christmas lights, decorated trees, or any resemblance of the holiday season at all. Many people are working in their offices, stores are open, and children are in school. However, two major cities in this region, Bethlehem and Jerusalem, celebrate the holiday season with great religious grandeur, as they are part of the Holy Land and the place of Jesus Christ's birth.

Christmas in Bethlehem is a festive display of twinkling lights and holiday cheer. Every home has an elaborate nativity scene. Any Christian home in Bethlehem has a cross painted on the front door.

Susan Rowsell

One of the most treasured Christmas traditions in Bethlehem is the Christmas Eve parade. Thousands of tourists watch the parade from doorways and the roof of the Basilica. The parade is headed by galloping horsemen alongside the police straddling Arabian horses. A man follows riding a black pony, as he carries a cross. He is followed by the church men and government executives. The parade travels through the streets of Bethlehem to the church, where an image of the Holy Child is placed. The church enters into a cave where a silver star represents the birthplace of Christ.

After the conclusion of the parade, families gather for a traditional Christmas Eve feast. Families enjoy turkey cooked with cinnamon, pepper, and nutmeg and stuffed with rice. They enjoy stuffing mixed with pine nuts and almonds. Families enjoy baklava and wheat porridge for dessert. The Holy Land of Bethlehem illuminates during the Christmas season, as thousands of people from all over the world celebrate the birth of Christ and his empowering light of peace and goodwill to all mankind.

Christmas in Jerusalem

Merry Christmas

Christmas is very empowering in Jerusalem, and their Christmas celebrations incorporate family, kinship, and strength of family unity. The people of Jerusalem believe it is very important during the holiday season to pay homage to all their families and friends. In Jerusalem, they enjoy many family gatherings during the holiday season.

Homes are decorated with lights. Tables are festively decorated for entertainment. Each home is adorned with a Christmas tree. Bowls of freshly baked cookies are placed on tables throughout the home. Butter cookies and shortbread cookies are very popular holiday treats in Jerusalem. It is very customary in Jerusalem to compliment the hostess for her holiday decor. Christmas chocolates are served with rich liqueurs and wines. It is proper etiquette to eat any cookies or chocolates served. It is, however, socially acceptable to decline alcohol.

In Jerusalem, they have festive Christmas Eve celebrations honouring the birth of Christ. Families partake in a holiday feast and enjoy one another's company. Christmas in Jerusalem is all about family togetherness.

Merry Christmas, from Jerusalem; may you prosper in the company of those you love this holiday season.

The Story of the Candy Cane

A candy maker in Indiana wanted to make a candy that would remind people of the true meaning of Christmas. He made the candy cane to incorporate the symbols of the birth, ministry, and death of Jesus Christ. He began with a stick of pure white to symbolize the virgin birth and sinless nature of Jesus. The hardness of the candy cane symbolized the solid rock—the foundation of the church and the firmness of the promises of God.

The candy maker then shaped his cane into the form of a "J" to represent the precious name of Jesus. It also represented the staff of the good shepherd, who reaches down to reclaim the fallen lamb who, like his sheep, has gone astray.

Thinking the candy cane was somewhat plain, the candy maker stained it with red stripes. He used three small stripes to show the stripes of the scourging Jesus received. The large red stripe was for the blood shed by Christ on the cross so that we could have the promise of eternal life.

The Candy Cane

Look at the candy cane
What do you see?

Susan Rowsell

Stripes that are red
Like the blood shed for me.

White is for my Saviour
Who is sinless and pure
"J" is for Jesus, my Lord that's for sure.

Turn it around
And a staff you will see
Jesus, my shepherd, was born for me!

Author Unknown

Christmas in Iceland

Gleðileg Jól

Christmas in Iceland is known as Yule or *Jól*. Long before Christianity was introduced, the people of Iceland celebrated the Winter Solstice with great grandeur. Hundreds of people would gather together in one's home and drink and feast all night long. Once Christianity was introduced to Iceland, they celebrated the birth of Christ during the holiday season.

In Iceland, Advent begins on the fourth Sunday before Christmas. Iceland becomes a twinkling winter wonderland of magic. Lights glow through the snow-laden trees. Musical concerts fill the crisp night air. The laughter of children brings excitement to the young and the old. One of the oldest traditions in Iceland is the lighting of the "Oslo" tree. A tall evergreen tree is decorated and displayed for all to see.

There are two Advent lights in Iceland. The Advent wreath consists of four candles; one for each of the Sundays of Advent. The other Advent light is a triangular-shaped candelabra that holds seven candles. The candelabra is placed in the front window of the home. Icelanders love to decorate for Christmas. Christmas trees are decorated on the first day of Advent. Homes are strewn with holiday lights. Store fronts, churches, schools, and city streets are aglow with holiday cheer. Þorláksmessa, named after a famous priest in Iceland, is celebrated on December 23rd. This is the last day that stores are open before Christmas. Holiday shoppers scurry about finishing their last-minute shopping. Christmas in Iceland is all about family and children. Adults do not drink alcohol during the Christmas festivities. Children enjoy a three-week holiday from school. The final day of classes in Iceland is a joyous occasion filled with festive activities. Children enjoy homemade baked goods and sing lots of Christmas carols.

The children of Iceland don't have just one gift bearer, they have thirteen. They are called Yule Lads. The Yule Lads are descendants of trolls. In ancient times, the Yule Lads came down from the mountains to scare children. Today, the Yule Lads are the gift bearers during the holiday season. Their names are: Sheep-Cote Clod, Gully Gawk, Stubby, Spoon-Licker, Pot-Licker, Bowl-Licker, Door-Slammer, Skyr-Gobbler, Sausage-Swiper, Window-Peeper, Doorway-Sniffer, Meat-Hook, and Candle-Stealer. Each child in Iceland puts their best shoe in the windowsill on December 12th, and each day of Christmas a different troll makes his way down the mountain and leaves a small gift in the shoe of each child. Some children have tried leaving a boot in their windowsill in hopes of receiving a larger gift, but these mischievous little trolls will not be fooled. Naughty children will find a rotten potato in their shoe. All of the Yule Lads wear red clothing and black boots and have long white beards.

Christmas dances are very popular in Iceland. Children love to gather together and sing and dance around the Christmas tree. The Yule Lads have been known to join in the fun, singing and dancing with the children. They often leave them a little goody bag upon their departure. The day after Christmas the first Yule Lad makes his way back up the mountain. The others follow one by one, with the last one leaving on January 6th—the final day of Christmas.

The ringing of the bell at the Lutheran Cathedral in Reykjavik announces the arrival of Christmas. The ringing of the bell symbolizes that people embrace one another and wish one another a Merry Christmas. Families then gather together for a festive feast. The festive meal consists of ham, smoked lamb with lots of vegetables, gravies and jams. After dinner families gather under the tree and exchange gifts. Many families spend a quiet evening reading books by the fireplace. Books are very popular gifts during the holiday season in Iceland. Iceland purchases and publishes more books per year per capita than any other country in the world. The majority of books are purchased between September and November. Book fairs are held in November, and families carefully choose their gift selections. The Icelanders tradition for giving books during the holiday season originated during World War II. During the war, paper was one of the few things that wasn't rationed. Books were affordable gifts during the holiday season.

New Year's Eve is a grand night of celebrations in Iceland. The firework displays are some of the most magnificent worldwide. At midnight, the fire trucks and harboured ships honk their horns to bring in the new year. New Year's Eve is all about the adults. Many of the adults spend the evening at the local pubs and clubs, dancing and drinking the night away.

And when the holidays have ended and all the decorations have been taken down, the Icelanders reflect on the long bright days of the holiday season and settle in for the long winter months ahead.

Warm, cosy wishes for the holiday season, from Iceland.

Susan Rowsell

Christmas in Argentina

Feliz Navidad

In Argentina, Christmas is called "*La Navidad.*" Christmas Day is celebrated on December 25th, and the festivities and decorations begin in late November. Homes are beautifully decorated with lights, wreaths, and red, gold and white flowers. Red and white garland is hung around the doors of homes and shops. Because the weather is warm in Argentina during the holiday season, seasonal flowers are used to decorate. The Christmas tree is adorned with ornaments, small figurines of Christmas characters, and cotton balls to represent snow. Streets and shops are illuminated by electrical lights and shiny bulbs to reflect the holiday spirit throughout the country.

Almost every home in Argentina will have a nativity scene displayed underneath the Christmas tree. Most Christmas trees are decorated on December 8th, the day of the Feast of Immaculate Conception. This feast honours the virgin Mary.

Christmas Eve is the most anticipated night of the year in Argentina. Firework displays light the night sky. *Globos* are paper balloons that are lit from the inside and released into the starlit sky. A grand feast is served. The feast consists of roast turkey, roast pork stuffed with tomatoes, and lots of trimmings. Christmas bread and pudding are festive desserts enjoyed on Christmas Eve. *Niños envueltos* is a very traditional dish in Argentina. This dish consists of rolled steak stuffed with hard boiled eggs, minced meat, and spices.

Santa Claus is known as *Papai Noel*, and he leaves presents for the children of Argentina on Christmas Eve. Gifts are opened at midnight and then families attend Mass.

Christmas Day is usually a relaxing day spent in the garden.

The Christmas season in Argentina ends on January 6th. Children leave their shoes in the garden. They fill their shoes with hay and water for the magi. In the morning, they will find their shoes filled with holiday treasures.

Christmas in Argentina is a blend of religious and traditional customs. It is a time for love, peace and goodwill, getting together with family, and bringing good tidings to others.

Felices Fiestas, happy holidays, from Argentina.

Christmas in Belgium

Vrolijk Kerstfeest ~ Frohe Weihnachten

Christmas in Belgium is a grand winter celebration. Celebrations begin with the start of Advent. Advent wreaths and crowns are made from leylandii and greenery. Wreaths are hung on doors with four candles. One candle is lit on each of the four Sundays of Advent to countdown the coming of Jesus.

Homes, towns, store fronts, and public buildings are decorated with Christmas flair. Streets are lined with fairy lights. Life-size nativity scenes are displayed in gardens all across the country. Churches also display large nativity scenes. Many churches use live animals in their nativity scenes.

Christmas markets in Belgium are even more elaborate than those in Germany. Shoppers can browse through a large selection of cheeses, sausage, chocolates, and Christmas crafts and plants.

Ice sculpture contests are very popular in Belgium.

Winterland Hasselt is a magical winter wonderland of fun for the Belgians. There is a large ice rink for family skating and a Ferris wheel for children to take turns trying to touch the sky. Santa has a cosy home tucked in the woods where children can visit and sit with him. Santa often joins the kids at the café for hot cocoa and cookies.

Some Belgium children receive a visit from both St. Nicholas and Santa Claus. Children leave their boots by the fireplace. They leave out treats of tangerines, gingerbread chocolate, or cookies for St. Nicholas, his horse, and his mischievous partner, Black Peter. Black Peter climbs down the chimney to leave presents for the children of Belgium.

Towns all across Belgium host a St. Nicholas parade during the month of December. St. Nicholas visits schools and sporting events. He enjoys reading to children and cheering the kids on at their sports games.

Christmas Eve is a time for family reflection. Families enjoy early afternoon appetisers, commonly mini pizzas and soups. The main dinner consists of seafood, turkey, chicken, and assorted vegetables and gravies. Families enjoy the traditional Christmas log for dessert. Families exchange gifts on Christmas morning.

Families enjoy another festive meal on New Year's Eve. Children get spoiled with more presents. It is customary to receive three kisses on the cheek at the stroke of midnight. Children write a letter to their parents expressing their wishes for the coming year. They read these letters to their parents on New Year's Day.

The holiday festivities in Belgium end on January 6th, with the celebration of Epiphany. The children go door to door singing Christmas carols. They are rewarded with small homemade treats. Traditionally families enjoy a Three Wise Men pie, with a gold paper crown on top. A bean is hidden inside the pie. Whoever gets the bean gets to wear the crown for the day.

Holiday greetings, from Belgium.

Susan Rowsell

Christmas in Romania

Craciun Fericit

Romania is a festival of family fun activities. The season's festivities begin on December 6th when all of the children get to celebrate St. Nicholas Day. Children leave their shoes or boots out in hopes that St. Nicholas will fill them with gifts and treats. If it snows on December 6th, it is believed that St. Nicholas has shaken his beard so that winter will begin.

December 20th is known as *"Ziua de Ignat"* Day. It is tradition on this day for the head of the household to slaughter one of his pigs. Families then share a meal known as "Pork's Charity." Pieces of pork are cooked in a cauldron and served in a garlic sauce. The remaining pork is used for the Christmas meal. Ignatius Day is celebrated in honour of Saint Ignatius.

The excitement of Christmas really begins on Christmas Eve. Families gather together and decorate the Christmas tree. Children then go door to door singing Christmas carols. Children receive a little candies and chocolates, fruits, and traditional holiday cakes called *"cozonaci."*

A very traditional Christmas carol in Romania is called the "Star Carol." Children make a star out of coloured paper and decorate it with foil and bells. They then place the star on a pole. A picture of Baby Jesus or a nativity scene is placed in the centre of the star. The children take their stars with them when they go carolling.

In many regions of Romania, it is still traditional to have a band made of unmarried men sing Christmas carols from home to home. Band members usually play the drums, the saxophone, and the violin. They also receive small gifts for spreading Christmas cheer.

Santa Claus is known as *Moş Crăciun*, "Old Man Christmas." Old Man Christmas delivers presents on Christmas Eve. Traditional Christmas feasts are another intricate part of the holiday celebrations in Romania. Traditional foods include roast gammon, pork chops, sour vegetable soup, meatballs, and cabbage leaves stuffed with pork. Rich desserts include fruit bread, doughnuts, and cheese cake. Families enjoy singing Christmas carols all through the night.

New Year's Eve is called "Little Christmas" and is celebrated with great grandeur. The Romanians celebrate with hopes for good health and prosperity for the coming year.

May good health and prosperity be bestowed on you and yours, from Romania.

Susan Rowsell

Christmas in Italy

Buon Natale

The celebration of Christmas in Italy is a blend of Christianity and the ancient celebrations of Epiphany. Christmas celebrations begin eight days before Christmas and end with the Feast of Epiphany. The official Christmas season in Italy begins on the first day of Advent. This celebration is called "*Novena.*" On the first day of Novena, families set up beautiful nativity scenes in their homes. Italians were the founders of the nativity scene. During the holiday season, families gather around the nativity scene every morning and pray and light candles. Nativity scenes are very elaborate in Italy. Italy is home to one of the largest nativity scenes in the world, with over 600 objects.

During the holiday season, children sing holiday songs at the homes of carpenters in honour of St. Joseph. Musical salutes are performed to honour the virgin Mary.

Children write letters to their parents wishing them a Merry Christmas. They promise to behave nicely during the holiday season. They make a list of gifts they would like to receive. Their letters are read out loud at the dinner table.

In some regions of Italy, children celebrate St. Nicholas Day. In other regions, children receive gifts from *Babbo Natale,* and some Italian children receive their gifts from *Befana.*

Most families like to keep the Yule log burning throughout the Christmas season. Many families sing the Shepherd's Carol throughout the holiday. This song is a dedication to the shepherds who came during Advent and went from home to home playing their bagpipes and spreading the news of the Saviour's birth.

Christmas Eve begins when the first star appears in the night sky. Families light candles outside their homes to welcome the Holy Family. The Yule log burns to drive evil spirits away and to provide warmth for the baby Jesus. The Italians don't eat during the day, as it is a fast day. They enjoy a lavish meal after Midnight Mass. The festive meal consists of roasted eel, seafood, pastas, vegetables, salads, and breads. They enjoy many Christmas sweets, including gingerbread prepared with hazelnuts, almonds, and honey. They also enjoy cakes filled with candies and fruits. During the meal, a large ornamental bowl is passed around the table and each family member receives a gift.

The Christmas season ends on January 6th. For many Italian children, this is the day they receive their long-awaited Christmas treasures. A special cake is made to honour Befana.

Holiday greetings, from Italy.

Hanukkah

The Festival of Lights

Hanukkah is the Jewish festival of lights. This celebration honours the rededication of the second Jewish temple in Jerusalem. Hanukkah begins on the 25th of Kislev. The Jewish use a lunar calendar, so the dates of Hanukkah vary from year to year. Hanukkah can be celebrated anytime from late November to late December.

Around 200 BC, Israel was ruled under Greek law; however, the king allowed his people to practise their own religious beliefs. In 171 BC, King Antiochus came into rule. He wanted his people to live by the Greek religion and worship all Greek gods. Most of the Jewish people wanted to continue to practise their own religious beliefs.

Menelaus was appointed to be the High Priest by King Antiochus. Menelaus was forced to flee Jerusalem during a riot. The king was furious and he took his anger out on the

Jewish people and the city of Jerusalem. Homes were burned down and thousands of Jewish people were killed. Many others were forced into slavery. Antiochus then attacked the Jewish temple. The Jewish temple was the most sacred building in Israel to the Jewish people. Antiochus put a statue of the Greek God Zeus in the centre of the Jewish temple. The statue's face resembled Antiochus. On 25th of Kislev, Antiochus destroyed the most holy place inside the temple and destroyed the Jewish holy scrolls.

Antiochus turned the Jewish temple into a shrine for Zeus. He banished the Jewish religion from being practised. Anyone who practised the Jewish religion was killed along with their family. Many Jewish people were killed because they refused to give up their beliefs.

Sometime later, a former Jewish priest named Mattathias was forced to make an offering to the statue of Zeus. He refused to do so and killed one of the king's soldiers. Mattathias and his sons went on to kill several other soldiers in the village. Mattathias died a short time later from old age. His sons stayed in hiding and continued to kill several other soldiers. After three years of fighting, they defeated the Syrian soldiers in open battle.

After winning the battle, they returned to Jerusalem. The Jewish people rebuilt their temple, completing their work on Kislev 25th, exactly three years after the statue of Zeus had been placed in the temple. The Jewish people rededicated their temple to God. A *menorah* was lit to celebrate the rededication of the temple. The miracle of Hanukkah is that one day's worth of oil lit the menorah for eight days.

The menorah is a sacred part of the Hanukkah celebrations. It is a candelabrum with eight branches and a central socket. The menorah is placed in the front window of a family's home so that it can be seen by people from the outside, much as people that celebrate Christmas display lights on the outside of their home. The menorah holds eight candles. The shamash is a special candle used to light one candle each night until all eight candles have been lit. Blessings are said after each candle is lit. The Jewish feel blessed to have won the right to follow their religious beliefs. For one hour after a candle is lit, work is forbidden. Families spend time teaching and learning the Jewish teachings. Families play traditional games and sing holiday songs. They also use this time to exchange gifts.

A customary family game during Hanukkah is a gambling game called "*dreidel*." There are four letters adorning the sides of the dreidel. The letters represent the first letters in "*Nes Gadol Haya Sham*," meaning "a great miracle happened there."

Latkes, a potato pancake, brisket, and jelly-filled donuts, are popular foods during the Hanukkah season.

Historically, Hanukkah was not a gift-giving celebration. Gift giving became more common as Jewish people became aware of the gift-giving celebrations of Christmas. Many Jewish families wanted to make the holiday celebrations more joyous for their children. The Jewish people celebrate Purim in the Spring, which is more their gift-giving celebration. During Hanukkah, children generally receive *gelt*. Gelts are gold-covered chocolate coins. These coins represent money; children give their coins to others as a form of charity. They are taught to share their wealth with others.

Hanukkah is celebrated in much the same way that Christmas is celebrated around the world. Families gather together with good food, good cheer, and good blessings. Their celebrations embrace the struggles and tribulations of their people. They celebrate and honour the freedom they fought for.

Happy Kwanzaa

Kwanzaa is an African American celebration that honours the heritage and identity of African American people. Kwanzaa is celebrated from December 26th to January 1st. Many African American people celebrate Christmas as well and incorporate Kwanzaa into their holiday celebrations.

Kwanzaa is derived from the phrase *"matunda ya kwanzaa,"* which means "first fruits." Just like Christmas, families celebrate the holiday differently around the world. But the basic principles remain the same: singing, dancing, drum playing, poetry reading, and of course, lots and lots of delicious foods.

The *kinara* is a special candle holder. The kinara holds seven candles. Many families place the kinara by their Christmas trees. The candles are lit one by one for the seven nights of Kwanzaa. The lighting of each candle represents the seven principles of Kwanzaa. The seven principles are called *"Nguzo Saba."* The seven principles of Kwanzaa represent the values of the African American people. Kwanzaa is celebrated to reinforce the principles of their culture and to maintain a strong community amongst themselves.

The first of the seven principles is *Umoja* (unity), striving to maintain unity in family, community, nation, and race.

The second principle is *Kujichagulia* (self-determination), working to define oneself and speak for oneself.

The third principle is *Ujima* (collective work and responsibility) to build and maintain the community, solving problems together and as if they are one's own.

The fourth principle is *Ujamaa* (cooperative economics), building and maintaining stores, shops, and other profitable businesses as a community.

The fifth principle is *Nia* (purpose), collectively building and developing the community in order to restore its people to their traditional greatness.

The sixth principle is *Kuumba* (creativity), collectively doing as much as one can, in a way that one can, in order to leave the community more beautiful and beneficial than when it was inherited.

The final principle is *Imani* (faith), believing in the people, parents, teachers and leaders that make up one's community, and the righteousness and victory of their struggles.

There are also seven symbols represented in the celebration of Kwanzaa.

The first of the seven symbols is *Mazao*: the crops of fruits, nuts, and vegetables, symbolizing the foundation of the Kwanzaa celebrations. The crops represent the historical gathering of the African American people during harvest. Joy, sharing, unity, and thanksgiving are the fruits of collective planning and work.

The second symbol is *Mkeka*. The mkeka is a place mat made from straw or cloth. The mkeka symbolizes the tradition of the African American people to stand on and build their lives. The African American people believe today stands on their yesterdays.

The third symbol is *Muhindi*. Muhindi is an ear of corn. The stalk of corn represents fertility. Fertility symbolizes that children bring life to the future hopes of the family.

The fourth symbol is *Mishumaa saba*. The mishumaa saba are the seven candles. Candles are ceremonial objects with two primary purposes. The purposes of the seven candles are to recreate the sun's power and to provide the light. The illuminating fire of the candles is a basic element of the universe. Every African American celebration includes some form of fire. Fire is mystique like the sun and create or destroy.

The fifth symbol is *Kinara*. The kinara is the candle holder. The kinara is the centre of the Kwanzaa setting and represents the original stalk from which they came. In African American festivals ancestors are always remembered and honoured.

The sixth symbol is *Kikombe cha umoja*, the unity cup. The unity cup is a special cup used to perform the libation ritual during the karamu feast. The feast takes place on the sixth day of Kwanzaa. The unity cup is passed around the table. Everyone sips from the cup. The oldest person then pours the drink in the direction of the four winds to honour the ancestors.

The final symbol is *Zawadi*, the gifts. Imani is celebrated on the seventh and final day of Kwanzaa. Meaningful gifts are exchanged to encourage growth, self-determination, achievement and success. Children are given gifts to reward their accomplishments and for keeping their commitments. Gifts are usually homemade. A substantial amount of time is put into making gifts. Accepting a gift implies a moral obligation to fulfil the promise of the gift.

Symbolic colours of red, green, and black from the flag represent African Gods. Red is the colour of Shango, the God of Fire, Lightning, and Thunder. He represents the struggle for self-determination and freedom. Black is the people and the earth—the source of life. Green represents the earth that sustains and provides hope, employment, and the fruits of the harvest.

The feast on the last night of Kwanzaa is an elaborate display of dishes, including African creole, Cajun catfish, jerk chicken, groundnut stew, rice, collard greens, Kwanzaa slaw, grits, beans, and okra.

The table is laden with the colours and symbols of the Kwanzaa celebration.

Kwanzaa is a unique way of connecting the spirit and Yuletide blessings of Christmas into the heritage and culture of the African American people. A celebration incorporating the joy of family, freedom, prosperity, and hope.

December 12th

Christmas in Ireland

Nollaig Shona

Christmas in Ireland is celebrated in a very religious manner. The holiday festivities begin on December 8th, with the Feast of Immaculate Conception. Schools are closed for the day. Families enjoy spending the day together ice skating. It is the biggest shopping day of the year. Many families begin decorating their homes for the holidays. It is bad luck in Ireland for the Irish to begin their decorating before December 8th.

The Irish love to decorate with holly and berries. Decorating with holly during the holiday season is a tradition that began in Ireland. Holly was a plant that flourished during the Christmas season in Ireland, and even the poor could afford to decorate their homes with holly. The Irish believe that the more berries you use for decorating, the more good luck will come your way in the coming year: "May the luck of the Irish be with us all in the year to come." The Irish love to decorate their Christmas trees with tinsel and lights and bright coloured balls. A Christmas crib is nestled beneath the tree where the presents are laid.

The Irish are very traditional in honouring the dead during the holiday season. Graves are decorated with holly and ivy, and prayers are said for the dead during Midnight Mass.

During the holiday season, the women of the household make a seed cake for each member of the family. They make three puddings, one for each day of Epiphany: Christmas Day, New Year's Day, and the Twelfth Night.

On Christmas Eve, families enjoy a festive meal of turkey, spiced beef, goose, ham, vegetables, and puddings. When the Christmas Eve meal is finished, the table is set with a loaf of bread filled with seeds and raisins. A large candle is lit and placed in the front window. This is a symbol of welcome to Mary and Joseph to seek warmth and shelter. The candle's light is a beacon to offer warmth and shelter to any wandering travellers. Families enjoy singing Christmas carols. Many families attend Midnight Mass. Children hang their stockings for Santa Claus. Santa Claus is known as *San Nioclás* in Ireland. Children leave him a piece of mince pie and a bottle of Guinness.

Gifts are exchanged on Christmas morning. Families enjoy singing Christmas carols around the Christmas tree. Some of the Irish jump into the cold sea waters to raise money for charity.

St. Stephen's Day is celebrated on December 26th. In some regions of Ireland, the Wren Boys Procession still takes place. Young boys dress in old clothing and blacken their faces. They go home to home carrying a pole with a holly bush. They sing Christmas carols in exchange for food and money. In ancient times, a wren was killed and carried around on a holly bush. The wren has a very loud song and is sometimes known as "the king of the birds." People went door to door singing Christmas carols in exchange for money to feed the hungry wren. Irish men also like to play football and watch horse races on St. Stephen's Day.

The Feast of Epiphany is still practised in some regions of Ireland. The women get the day off from all household chores. The men do all the chores and prepare the meals. The women get together to sew and eat and gossip. Many Irish women would like this tradition to remain a part of the holiday celebrations in Ireland.

"With ivy, shamrock and bright holly berry, be Christmas to you all blessed and Merry!" Happy Christmas to you, from Ireland.

Susan Rowsell

Christmas in Norway

God Jul

Christmas in Norway begins with the celebration of the St. Lucia ceremony on December 13th. At daybreak, the youngest daughter from each family puts on a white robe with a sash and wears a crown adorned with evergreens and white candles. The boys dress up as star boys, wearing white shirts and long pointed hats. The children then wake up their parents and serve them coffee and St. Lucia buns.

After the St. Lucia ceremony, families decorate the Christmas tree. Trees are decorated with candles or white lights, flags, apples, straw ornaments, glass balls, tinsel, and colourful paper bags made by the children in the family. The Christmas tree is traditionally decorated by the children in the family, as it is believed to bring good luck to the family in the coming year.

Traditionally every Christmas, the Norwegians give the people of the United Kingdom a giant Christmas tree to thank them for their help during World War II. The tree stands in Trafalgar Square, London. Thousands of people come annually to the tree lighting ceremony every December.

During Advent, kids like to countdown the days until Christmas. In some regions of

Norway, children countdown the days of Christmas with a chocolate calendar. In other regions, children receive a small gift for every day of Advent. These gifts are called *Adventsgaver*.

Yule lunches are very popular during the holiday season in Norway. Friends and family arrange dinner parties and enjoy kinship, good food, and lots of wine.

The biggest night of the year in Norway is Christmas Eve. At noon, a special rice pudding is served at the dining room table. A small almond is hidden inside the pudding. The family member that eats the almond receives a small chocolate treat. Families attend an afternoon church service and enjoy singing Christmas hymns. At five o'clock, the church bells ring, announcing the arrival of Christmas. Families read a story from the Bible. Families then partake in the Christmas Eve meal. The festive meal consists of pork rib, pieces of lamb steamed over birch branches, poached cod, and an assortment of stuffing and vegetables. The Norwegians love their beer and Aquauit during the holiday celebrations. A special drink called "*julebrus*" is made for children. It is a sweet and fizzy red drink. Families enjoy a traditional Christmas dessert of rice blended with whipped cream and red sauce.

Norway does not have a traditional Santa Claus. Norway have *Nisse*. There is *fjønisse*, who takes care of the barn animals. He is short and wears wool clothing and a red knitted hat. He lives in the barn. If he is not given a bowl of Christmas porridge on Christmas Eve, he will create mischief. He will turn out the lights in the barn and move the animals around. *Julenissen* is the Christmas Nisse. He delivers presents to the boys and girls of Norway on Christmas Eve. He delivers his presents in person.

On Christmas Day, families invite friends and family for a festive brunch. They enjoy a rich meal with lots of beer and homemade cakes, cookies, nuts, and dates. The

Norwegians like to light a candle on each night from Christmas Eve to New Year's Eve. The Norwegians bring in the coming year with great flair and lots and lots of beer.

Cheers to the coming year, from Norway.

December 13th

Christmas in Africa

Rehus-Beal-Ledeats

Christmas in Africa is celebrated differently throughout the country. Christmas in the Congo begins with the annual Christmas Pageant. Homes in the Congo are decorated with pine branches and locally grown flowers. The Christmas tree stands in the corner of the home, dressed with many homemade beaded decorations. Presents are put around the tree for the children of the family. Children hang their stockings to be filled by Father Christmas.

Christmas Day in the Congo begins with carollers walking through the villages past the homes of missionaries, singing well-known Christmas carols. Many people are awakened Christmas morning to the lovely Christmas hymns as the carollers pass their homes. Everyone then dresses in their most formal wear and prepares their offerings for the Christmas Day services. The most important part of the service is the gift that is brought for Baby Jesus. Everyone who attends the service will lay down a gift for the baby Jesus on the communion table. After service, families will gather together for a festive meal. In the Congo, the festive meal consists of turkey or roast beef, mince pies, suckling pig, yellow rice with raisins, vegetables, and plum pudding. Most homes across Africa decorate the family table with festive decor. Families enjoy pulling Christmas crackers and wearing the paper crowns while enjoying their meal.

In Ghana, on Africa's west coast, churches and homes are decorated for the holiday season on the first day of Advent. They are decorated with evergreens or palm trees laden with candles. The Christmas season in Ghana coincides with the cocoa harvest. Everyone returns home from the fields and mountains to partake in the holiday celebrations. The Christmas season in Ghana is a time to give appreciation for one another's wealth and good fortune. On Christmas Eve, children march the streets singing Christmas carols to announce that Christ is near. In the evening, families attend Mass. Children participate in nativity plays and families sing Christmas hymns together. Families travel home and children hang their stockings by the fireplace in anticipation of the arrival of Father Christmas. Children open their gifts on Christmas morning. On Christmas Day, children and elderly people flock to the fields singing Christmas carols, representing the angels in the fields of Bethlehem.

In Liberia, on the west coast of Africa, most homes have an oil palm tree that is decorated with bells. Christmas carols are sung on Christmas morning to wake families up for a festive day of family activities. Gifts of soap, cotton, cloth, sweets, pencils, and books are exchanged in family households. Families attend morning church services and sing Christmas hymns. Christmas Day dinner is enjoyed outside under the bright, sunny skies. Families sit in a circle and enjoy a meal of rice, beef, and biscuits.

Families enjoy outdoor games and activities. The festivities end with spectacular fire-work displays.

Across Africa, Christmas Day is spent in the great outdoors in the unity of the family circle.

May the light of the season be with you; holiday greeting, from Africa.

Susan Rowsell

Christamas in Indonesia

Selamat Natal

In Indonesia, both Christians and non-Christians bond together to celebrate Christmas as a united unit. Shopping malls and markets are decorated with trees and wreaths. In Bali Island, Christmas trees are made from feathers. These famous trees have been exported to countries all over the world. The Javanese tree is decorated with paper and other recyclable materials. In 2011, a hotel in Indonesia displayed a Christmas tree decorated with edible chocolates for their guests. Hotels throughout Indonesia decorate for the holiday season with towering trees and lavishly decorated Christmas wreaths. Hotels host festive beach parties and jubilant Christmas Eve parties.

In Jakarta, communities hold Christmas parties for children. Santa Claus is the honorary guest, and he reads the children Christmas stories and hands out presents and sweets. There are parades complete with marching bands and carollers in many regions across Indonesia. Almost all of the schools in Indonesia host Christmas parties for the children. The children partake in crafts, games, and holiday baking and receive visits from Santa Claus. Santa Claus is very popular to the children of Indonesia.

Christmas markets are very popular. Many families do the majority of their holiday shopping at the local markets. Tourists from all over the world spend the holiday season in Indonesia, attracted by the crystal blue waters and warm summer days. Tourists enjoy the unique holiday gifts that can be found at the Christmas markets in Indonesia, including the beautiful flower arrangements that are locally made.

Christmas Eve is a magical night in Indonesia. Christmas spreads the word of God and celebrates the birth of Christ. Many families attend Midnight Mass. Churches are decorated with beautiful nativity scenes, and children enjoy acting out the Christmas story for their parents. Families enjoy singing Christmas hymns. Families enjoy a festive meal at home, on the beach, or at a local resort. The festive meal consists of *brenebon* soup, grilled pork, vegetables, and gravies. Families enjoy lots of festive cookies and cakes. *Nastar* are butter cookies filled with pineapple jam. Other holiday favourites are cheese cookies and "Snow White" cookies. Families also enjoy firework displays as they enjoy the mild evening air. Santa Claus leaves presents for the children of Indonesia on Christmas Eve.

Families open presents on Christmas morning and exchange cards. Families love to sing Christmas carols and dance and eat the day away.

Merry Christmas, from Indonesia.

Christmas in Denmark

Glaedeligh Jul

Denmark is a Scandinavian country in Europe. Christmas in Denmark is celebrated with deep Christian traditions and customs. The Christmas celebrations can begin as early as November. Families enjoy festive parties from the beginning of November through to Christmas Eve. Friends, neighbours, and relatives enjoy the holiday get-togethers. They partake in festive activities and enjoy homemade gingerbread and vanilla cookies. Many Denmark residents also enjoy holiday luncheons at work.

In Denmark, they begin decorating for the holiday season at the start of Advent. The Advent wreath is made from twigs and decorated with red berries and spruced cones. The wreath holds four candles. Advent wreaths are hung from the ceiling. Most families have an Advent candle. *Pakkekalender* is an Advent gift calendar for the children to countdown the days of the holiday season. Children receive a small gift on each day of Advent. In

Denmark, there is also a special television program for children during Advent. A different holiday cartoon or movie is aired on each day of Advent.

Christmas trees are decorated for the holiday season. Most Christmas trees have Yule hearts, brightly coloured bulbs, and fairy hair that makes the branches of the tree glitter. A gold or silver star sits atop the tee. Paper star lanterns are hung outside of homes.

St. Lucia Day is celebrated on December 13th. St. Lucia was a third-century martyr who brought food to Christians in hiding. The eldest girl in each family portrays St. Lucia by wearing a white robe and a crown of candles. Daughters serve their parents saffron buns and coffee or mulled wine.

There is a huge holiday celebration at Tivoli Gardens. The park is filled with lights and thousands of decorated Christmas trees. There are hundreds of vendors selling baked goods and wines. Children can visit with Santa and have their picture taken.

Every December, Denmark launches a special series of Christmas stamps called *"julemaerket."* These stamps are purchased to send Christmas cards. All the proceeds are donated to charity.

December 23rd marks the beginning of the grand celebrations of the holiday season. Families enjoy a large feast. Families relax by the fire enjoying cinnamon rice pudding.

Christmas Eve is the biggest celebration of the year in Denmark. The Christmas Eve feast consists of roast goose, duck, or pork with potatoes, red cabbage, and cranberry jam. Dessert is rice pudding with whipped cream and almonds. Many families enjoy an evening stroll and feed the forest animals. Families enjoy Christmas carols around the Christmas tree. Parents enjoy a Christmas snap or two.

Santa Claus is known as *Julemanden*, the "Yule Man." Julemanden has elves called "*julenissers.*" Julenissers live in attics and barns to watch over children to see who is being naughty or nice. Julemanden and his julenissers love rice pudding. Children leave out saucers of milk or rice pudding on Christmas Eve. Many families attend Midnight Mass.

Families enjoy a modest lunch on Christmas Day, consisting of open-face sandwiches and Danish cupcakes. Families exchange gifts in the evening and end the holiday season in song.

Holiday greetings, from Denmark.

Susan Rowsell

Christmas in Greenland

Juullimi Pilluarit ~ Glaedelig Jul

Greenland is a beautiful country within the Kingdom of Denmark. Christmas came to Greenland in the 1700s by Christian missionaries. There are two prominent languages in Greenland, Inuit and Danish. Christmas in Greenland is a magically important celebration for Greenlanders.

Nestled in the icy slopes of Greenland are the villages of the polar Inuit. Families love to visit friends and relatives during the holiday season. Throughout the month of December, friends and relatives enjoy luncheons with coffee and holiday cakes. Gifts are exchanged throughout the season. Traditional gifts include model sledges, polished walrus tusks, and sealskin mittens. Christmas in Greenland brings communities together. Everyone is included in the celebrations, and everyone receives gifts. Children love going door to door singing Christmas carols and spreading Christmas cheer.

Trees do not grow in Greenland; Christmas trees are imported from Denmark. The people of Greenland believe deeply in the earth and all it provides. Greenlanders use all the parts of an animal and every piece of nature in their region. Some Greenlanders use a driftwood tree decorated with heather. Christmas trees are decorated with candles, paper hats, and lots of brightly coloured ornaments. Some families wait until the evening of December 23rd to decorate their trees.

It is customary for villagers to put up beautifully decorated trees on nearby hills so that everyone can enjoy the spirit of Christmas. Christmas village trees are decorated at the beginning of Advent.

The star is a very important symbol for Greenlanders during the holiday season. The star of Christmas is a symbol of Jesus Christ's birth. Stars are lit on the first day of Advent. Many Greenlanders attend church on the four Sundays of Advent. Orange illuminated stars are hung in homes and public buildings. Christmas in Greenland occurs in winter, and the sun never comes out. The stars bring light during the holiday season.

Some Greenlanders still practise the tradition of leaving lights in the graveyards. A small cove of snow is built atop the grave to keep the candles from burning out. The lights cast a majestic glow amongst the white blanket of snow.

The St. Lucia's parade is a cherished custom celebrated in Greenland. St. Lucia parades are performed at schools and day care institutions. Children dress in white robes carrying a candle. St. Lucia leads the parade wearing a wreath holding four candles. Children lead parades through hospitals and old age homes.

Christmas Eve is a jubilant night of singing, dancing, and eating. The Christmas Eve feast consists of reindeer, halibut, seal, whale steak, pork roast, and duck. Families enjoy a festive cake made with mulled homemade wine. Men often serve women on Christmas Eve.

The children of Greenland believe Santa and Mrs. Claus live in the northern part of

Greenland, in Spraglebugten. Santa's sleigh is pulled by dogs. Santa Claus brings lots of cheer to the children of Greenland on Christmas Eve.

May the Christmas star fill your home with hope this holiday season. Season's greetings, from Greenland.

Christmas in Spain

Feliz Navidad

In Spain, Christmas is known as *Navidad*. Christmas in Spain begins on December 8th, with the Feast of Immaculate Conception. This feast is a religious celebration honouring the immaculate conception of the Virgin Mary. All businesses, schools, and stores are closed across the country. Families decorate their homes for the holiday season. Christmas trees are decorated and nativity scenes are displayed underneath the tree.

Christmas markets are very popular in the country of Spain. You can find fruits, desserts, gifts, and flowers at these traditional markets. During the Christmas season, families assemble a model manger with carved figurines of the Holy Family, the Three Wise Men, shepherds, and angels. Families gather around the nativity scene and sing, while the children dance and play the tambourine. The cow is an animal of great respect in Spain; the breath of the cows kept the baby Jesus warm after his birth.

On December 22nd, there is a Christmas lottery called "*El Gordo.*" People buy tickets in hopes of winning the large grand prize. Smaller prizes are given out as well. The Christmas lottery symbolizes pride and prestige for the Spanish people.

In Spain, Christmas Eve is called "*Noche Buena,*" which means "good night." On Noche Buena, the Spanish light oil lamps, and when the church bells ring, they walk to Midnight Mass by the light of their lamps. The Mass of the Rooster is held at midnight. It is said that the only time a rooster crowed at midnight was on the night the baby Jesus was born. The most beautiful church service in Spain is held at the Abbey of Montserrat, high in the mountains near Barcelona. After Mass, families travel home by the light of their lamps and the stars in the sky. They enjoy a Christmas toast and champaign. They sing and dance around the Christmas tree all night long. Some families exchange presents. In Spain, Noche Buena is a good night, not a night for sleeping.

On Christmas Day, swing sets are set up in courtyards and children swing and sing the day away. Families enjoy festive meals and lots of holiday desserts.

Children receive their presents on the day of Epiphany. Children write letters to the Three Kings (the Three Wise Men) on December 26th asking for toys, story books, and clothing. On the eve of Epiphany, they leave their shoes by the door. The Three Wise Men fill them with sweets and gifts. Epiphany Day is filled with parades, singing, dancing, and gift giving. Families enjoy a feast as they conclude the holiday celebrations for the year.

Merry Christmas from the bottom of our hearts, from Spain.

Susan Rowsell

Christmas in Mexico

Feliz Navidad

The Mexicans celebrate Christmas with great Spanish flair. Homes are decorated with poinsettias, which are native to Mexico. During the month of December, Mexico is a grand festival of markets, holiday décor, and strings and strings of twinkling lights. Christmas markets are full of stalls that display cheese, cookies, crafts, and bundles and bundles of poinsettias.

Christmas in Mexico is a jubilant affair. From tequila shots to turkey tacos, people celebrate the holiday with great flair and joy.

Las Posadas is celebrated nine days before Christmas. When Mary and Joseph were looking for shelter before the birth of Baby Jesus, they were turned away from eight inns. They finally found an inn that would take them in on the ninth day of their travels. For nine days, children go door to door asking for shelter. At each door, families sing carols with them about Mary and Joseph and then send them on their way. On the ninth day, they are invited inside the home for shelter. They enjoy a lavish meal and sing carols and share prayers. They set up a nativity scene for the baby Jesus. Many families then gather together to watch a spectacular show of fireworks in the calm night sky.

Christmas Eve in Mexico is a very surreal and traditional night. Walkways, homes, stores, and streets are lined with brown paper lanterns called *"luminarias."* These lanterns are only lit on Christmas Eve. All electric lights in cities and towns all across the country are turned off on Christmas Eve. All motorized traffic is prohibited. Everyone walks by the light of the lanterns. The light of the lanterns leads the townspeople to Midnight Mass. After Midnight Mass, a large firework display announces the arrival of Christmas.

In some regions of Mexico, children receive their presents on Christmas Eve. In other regions of Mexico, children receive their presents on Three Kings' Day.

Mexicans that celebrate Christmas on Christmas Eve enjoy a festive feast after Midnight Mass. The meal consists of cod fish wrapped cornmeal dumplings and salad. *Biscochito* cookies are a traditional holiday favourite during the festivities. They are a shortbread cookie with a taste of cinnamon. The biscochito became the official state cookie of Mexico in 1989. Baby Jesus leaves presents for children on Christmas Eve. Mexican Christmas trees always have an angel perched on top of the tree. The largest angel ever made was in Mexico, by a man named Sergio Rodriguez in 2001. The angel was made out of a total of 2,496 beer bottles. The angel was almost nineteen feet tall and had a wingspan of eleven feet.

Other Mexicans celebrate Christmas on Epiphany Day, January 6th. A traditional cake, called the *"Rosca de Reyes,"* is made. A small figure of Baby Jesus is placed inside the cake. The person who receives the trinket in their piece of cake gets to be godparent to Baby Jesus at the Candelaria Celebrations on February 2nd. This is the final day of celebrations in Mexico.

May the light of the season be upon you this holiday season. *Feliz Navidad*, from Mexico.

Legend of the Poinsettia

In Mexico and in many other countries it is customary to bring a gift for the baby Jesus during the Christmas Eve Mass service. One legend tells the story of a young girl named Pepita. Pepita is a poor young girl whom is sad because she has no gift to bring the baby Jesus. Her cousin Pedro tries to cheer her up. He tells her that any gift will make the baby Jesus happy. Pepita picks up a handful of weeds and assembles them into a bouquet. At first she is embarrassed by her gift, but then she realizes that her gift comes from her heart and she is very pleased with her gift as she places it beneath the nativity scene. With everyone watching the weeds miraculously transform into beautiful red flowers. From that night on the poinsettia became known as 'Flores de Noche Buena.' Flowers of the Holy Night.' The moral of this story being that gifts from the heart are the best gifts of all.

Susan Rowsell

Christmas in Columbia

Feliz Navidad

In Columbia, Christmas celebrations begin on December 7th, with the Day of the Little Candles Celebration. Homes all across Columbia are decorated with candles and lights. Streets are lined with lanterns. There is music and dancing and lots of food and drinking. There are spectacular firework displays across the country. This celebration is on the eve of the Feast of Immaculate Conception, observed by the Catholics. This celebration is very popular across Columbia.

Families like to decorate their homes for the holiday season. Christmas trees are decorated with twinkling lights and shiny balls. Red and white candles are displayed in windows and strung on balconies. Nativity scenes are very popular in Columbia. In early December, children write letters to Baby Jesus with their Christmas wishes and place them in the nativity scene.

From December 16th until Christmas Eve, many Columbian families partake in Christmas Novena. Different families will host a gathering on each of these nights. Families and friends gather together for prayers and Christmas carolling and enjoy lots of festive foods and beverages.

The Christmas Eve meal is called "*Cena de Navidad.*" This meal consists of a variety of traditional dishes, including pork stuffed with rice and peas, ham, and turkey. Other festive favourites include cheesy fritters and fried pastries filled with sugar and jam. Columbians enjoy *natilla* for dessert, which is a set custard.

Many families attend Midnight Mass. They stay up all night long singing and dancing and enjoying the spirit of Christmas.

Christmas Day is a relaxing day for families. Families exchange presents and enjoy leftovers.

Columbians celebrate Holy Innocents' Day on December 28th. Families share jokes and play pranks on one another. Many Columbians enjoy watching bloopers on television. Families end the holiday season with some good old-fashioned laughter and cheer.

May laughter fill your home this holiday season; holiday greetings, from Columbia.

Susan Rowsell

Christmas in Brazil

Feliz Natal

Christmas in Brazil is the most important *dia de festa* of the year. Old Brazilian legend states that even the animals celebrate the birth of Christ through speech. The rooster says "*Cristo nasceu,*" which means Christ is born. The sheep say, "Belém da Judiéa," meaning at Bethlehem of Judea.

Brazil is a Portuguese-speaking country, and many of their Christmas traditions and customs are inspired by Portugal and Mexico.

In Brazil, towns and homes are decorated for the holiday season in early December. Homes and shops adorn beautiful evergreen trees dressed in colourful bulbs and lights. Nativity scenes are seen all throughout the cities and towns of Brazil. In Brazil, they are called "*Presépio,*" the manger where Baby Jesus slept in Bethlehem.

Throughout the month of December, Brazilians enjoy attending folk plays based on the stories of the shepherds. These plays are very unique and vary greatly from the traditional Christmas story. These stories are told by women who are accompanied by a Gypsy, who tries to kidnap the baby Jesus.

Many Brazilians take part in a secret Santa tradition during the month of December, called *"amigo secreto."* People exchange gifts throughout the month of December using a pretend name. Everyone reveals their secret name on Christmas Day.

For several decades, Brazilians have been receiving a thirteenth salary in December. Brazilians get double their pay in December. This money helps Brazilians do their holiday shopping; it also helps the prosperity of their economy. Brazilians are quite shocked that other countries don't partake in this tradition.

As part of the ancient traditions, Brazilians attend Midnight Mass, otherwise known as the Mass of the Rooster. The rooster announces the arrival of Christmas. Families then enjoy a festive meal called *"ceia."* The Christmas meal consists of roast turkey and pork, fresh vegetables, kale, garlic, and lots of festive cakes and pies. Children also enjoy lots and lots of ice cream.

Papai Noel lives in the icy backdrops of Greenland. He wears a red silk robe and carries a brown paper bag filled with presents. In some parts of Brazil, children leave a sock by the window. Papai Noel takes the sock and leaves a present in its place. Brazilians love to sing Christmas carols around the Christmas tree. "Silent Night" is a favourite Christmas carol.

On Christmas Day, families gather around the tree to exchange gifts. Many families enjoy a relaxing day at the beach.

The Christmas festivities end with the celebration of Epiphany. Brazilians honour the Three Wise Men and their quest to find the baby Jesus.

May the blessings of Christ be with you and yours this holiday season. Merry Christmas, from Brazil.

Susan Rowsell

Christmas in Austria

Frohe Weihnachten

Advent announces the arrival of the Christmas season in Austria. Most families hang the Advent wreath in their homes. The wreath holds four candles; one candle is lit on each of the four Sundays of Advent.

Christmas markets are popular in Austria. Vendors sell homemade decorations, gingerbread houses, baked goods, and wines.

St. Barbara Day is celebrated on December 4th, in dedication to St. Barbara. Small twigs from a cherry tree are placed in a vase. If flowers bloom by Christmas, family members will be blessed with good luck in the coming year.

Austrians like to decorate for the holidays with festive flair. Every town square in Austria displays a large evergreen tree dressed in colourful bulbs and lights. Some families wait to decorate their trees on Christmas Eve, while other families decorate their trees at the beginning of Advent. Some families light their tree for the first time on Christmas Eve. Christmas trees are decorated with gold and silver bulbs. Stars are made out of straw and placed atop the tree.

The twelve nights of the holiday season are called "*Rauhnachte*." Some families make a special holiday mixture during this time. It is a mixture of incense, palm branches, and herbals. Families spread this scent through their homes to keep evil spirits and misfortunes out of their homes.

Austrians love to sing Christmas carols, bake cookies, and decorate gingerbread houses during the holiday season. "Silent Night" was written in 1818 in Austria.

In ancient times, St. Nicholas was called *Krampus* in Austria. He was a big horned monster who wore rags and carried chains. He would punish naughty children. In present times, the *Christkind* delivers presents to the children of Austria. The Christkind is blond and wears wings and a halo. Children leave the window open so that she can fly into each home and leave gifts under the Christmas tree. The Christkind usually delivers presents while families are enjoying their Christmas Eve feast. This meal consists of carp fried in butter, vegetables, and potatoes. Austrians enjoy many festive desserts, including *weihnachtskekse* and *sachertorte*. *Weihnachtskekse* are traditional holiday cookies, and sachertorte is a traditional Christmas chocolate apricot cake. As families finish up the last crumbs of the feast, the Christkind rings her bell to let the anxious children know their presents are awaiting under the tree.

New Year's Eve is celebrated in cities and towns all across Austria. In Vienna, the capital city of Austria, there is a large musical concert. Families enjoy skiing and skating.

Epiphany Day is celebrated on January 6th in many regions of Austria. Families will mark their doors with chalk strokes to honour the Three Wise Men and bring good luck to their family and their home in the coming year.

May good luck be with you and yours this holiday season, from your friends in Austria.

Susan Rowsell

Christmas in Poland

The Christmas season in Poland begins with Advent. Christmas Day is celebrated on December 25th. One of the biggest traditions in Poland during the holiday season is cleaning the home for the holidays. The Polish women thoroughly clean their homes from top to bottom. It is believed that if the home is dirty for Christmas, it will remain dirty in the year to come.

During the holiday season, the women do a lot of holiday baking. *Pierniczki* are special ginger-bread cookies made in Poland. They are baked in various shapes, including stars and hearts. The Polish also like to make homemade ornaments, stars, and garland made from eggshells.

St. Nicholas is known as *Święty Mikołaj,* and he visits the children of Poland twice during the holiday season. Święty Mikołaj visits the Polish children on the eve of St. Nicholas Day. The children will find their boots filled with sweets and small gifts.

Christmas Eve is a very important and a very busy day in Poland. Christmas decorating begins very early in the morning. Evergreen boughs are placed around doorways. The ceilings of homes are decorated with *pająki*, a cobweb pattern. Colourful harvest wreaths, decorated with flowers and stars, are placed throughout the home. The Christmas tree stands in the living room and is decorated with homemade decorations of apples, chocolates, walnuts, paper chains, and candles. A star shines atop the tree.

Christmas Eve in Poland begins when the first star appears in the evening sky. The Christmas Eve feast is an elaborate meal. Hay or straw is placed under the white tablecloth. This is how maidens predict their future for the coming year. When supper has commenced, the maidens pull out blades of straw from under the tablecloth. A green blade of straw foretells marriage, a withered one signifies waiting for marriage, a yellow one signifies spinsterhood, and a short one foreshadows an early grave. An extra seat is always set at the table, as the Polish believe that no one should be alone on Christmas Eve. Any single person is welcome to join them for dinner.

In Poland, it is strongly believed that whatever happens on Christmas Eve will predict the future for the coming year. Arguments and hostility among family, friends, and neighbours is forbidden. A traditional Christmas Eve feast in Poland consists of twelve courses, representing the twelve apostles of Christ. Before dinner is served a special Christmas wafer, called "*oplatek*," is broken into pieces and shared among family members. This is considered to be a symbol of unity with Christ. A traditional Christmas meal consists of white carp, meatless cabbage rolls, noodles with poppy seeds, and lots of rich desserts and liqueurs. After dinner, families enjoy singing and dancing around the Christmas tree. Families then attend Midnight Mass. Święty Mikołaj visits the children while they are sleeping.

Christmas Day in Poland is known as "Little Star Day." Christmas Day is a quiet, restful day. Children open their presents and families gather together and reflect on the birth of Christ. No visitors are allowed to visit on Christmas Day. Housework, cleaning, and cooking are forbidden. Families enjoy eating leftovers.

St. Stephen's Day is the second holiday of Christmas. This is a day for visiting and exchanging Christmas greetings. On the evening of St. Stephen's Day, carollers go house to house singing Christmas carols. Young boys dress up and portray King Herod, a knight, a soldier, an angel, a devil, a Jew, and Mary and Joseph. They receive refreshments and small amounts of money.

In Poland, to portray the true spirit of Christmas, it is important to carry out the traditions of their ancestors during the Christmas season.

May the spirit of Christmas continue to shine year after year; season's greetings, from Poland.

Legend of the Christmas Spider

Legend tells the story of the poor widowed woman who could not afford to buy her children Christmas presents. She wanted her children to have a beautiful Christmas; even if she could not afford to buy them presents. After putting her children to bed, she went outside and cut down a tree and brought it inside. She decorated the tree with nuts and fruits and homemade decorations. She decorated the tree with lots of love, joy, and happiness. She cleaned her house until it was completely spotless. There wasn't a speck of dust or a cobweb to be seen. After so much hard work, she fell asleep exhausted. While she had been cleaning, the spiders had all fled to the attic; however, they were curious about the Christmas tree she had been decorating. So, the oldest and wisest spider gathered the others, and they all left the attic to see the beautiful Christmas tree. The tree was so huge and tall that the spiders could not see the decorations, so they climbed the tree, leaving trails of dull grey web behind them. Eventually, the entire tree was covered in dusty grey spider webs.

The Christ Child had seen what the spiders had done to the beautiful tree. He was happy that the spiders had been able to see the tree, but he worried that the mother would be upset to see her beautiful tree covered in dusty grey spider webs. So, he touched all the spider webs that covered the tree and turned them into gold and silver. The mother and her children woke up Christmas morning to see a beautiful Christmas tree dressed in silver and gold. This legend is still commemorated today, as people all over the world

Susan Rowsell

decorate their trees with tinsel. In some countries, families even place a spider figurine on their tree. It is a legend that shares the moral hard work and good intentions will be rewarded.

Christmas in Switzerland

Fröhlichi Weihnacht

Switzerland is a beautiful country in central Europe. The Christmas season in Switzerland begins with Advent. In some villages in Switzerland, families display life-size Advent calendars in their windows. Each family represents one of the twenty-four days of Advent. On each day of Advent, the represented family hosts a holiday party with good food and wine. These parties build the excitement of the holiday season for children.

During the month of December, men make torches out of poles. These torches light up the evening streets. Families enjoy sleigh rides and snowball fights under the light of the torches. Families like to walk by torch light into the woods to cut down their Christmas tree.

Susan Rowsell

Families hang a straw goat ornament in their homes. The goat guards the family home and ensures that the holiday festivities are joyous and cheerful.

Many Swiss families celebrate St. Lucia Day.

Christmas markets are very popular all across the country. Vendors sell an assortment of holiday decor, gifts, baked goods, sausages, and wines.

The Swiss enjoy spa days and holiday luncheons all through the month of December. Turkey, roast beef, salads, vegetables, and breads are favoured luncheon treats. Families love to bake Christmas cookies together. The Swiss love their cookies over the holiday season.

Christmas in Switzerland brings an array of colour, clanging cow bells, and glowing candles to inspire the holiday season and to ward off evil spirits during the dark, cold winter season.

December 24th is the Holy Night. The festive meal consists of ham and scalloped potatoes drizzled with cheese. Walnut cake is the traditional dessert. After dinner, the Christmas tree is revealed to the children. The tree is dressed with apples, bells, and Christmas shaped sugar cookies. Families share the Christmas story around the tree and sing Christmas hymns.

Santa Claus is known as *Samichlaus*. He wears a hooded red cape and a long robe. Samichlaus makes his entrance to Switzerland in early December. He has a partner named *Schmutzli*, little dirty one. Schmutzli's face is hidden behind a dark hooded cape. He punishes naughty children by swatting them with a broom. Samichlaus and Schmutzli usually travel by donkey. They deliver gifts on Christmas Eve. In Switzerland, children have to hunt for their presents.

Most families attend Midnight Mass. A belief is still held in many regions of Switzerland that animals were given the gift of speech on the very first Christmas. Animals are given an extra portion of grain on Christmas Eve, in gratitude, and also so that they won't talk. The Swiss believe that if you hear the animals talk on Christmas Eve, bad luck will be bestowed upon you in the coming year.

Christmas Day marks the beginning of the winter season in Switzerland. Many families head to the snow-capped mountains for some skiing. Other families like to go bobsledding or tobogganing. Some families take a vacation at one of the cosy ski resorts nestled in the mountains.

The *Urnäsch Silvesterkläuse* procession still takes place in regions across Switzerland. These processions are over two hundred years old. People dress in costume and go door to door singing, dancing, and playing instruments; wishing everyone a "Happy New Year."

The Swiss celebrate Epiphany Day. Children in Switzerland can receive gifts on St. Nicholas Day, New Year's Eve, and Epiphany Day. Samichlaus, Baby Jesus, Befana, and the Three Kings are all gift bearers in Switzerland. The children of Switzerland love the holiday season.

Ho ho ho and Merry Christmas, from Switzerland.

Susan Rowsell

Christmas in France

Joyeux Noël

France is an exquisite country to visit during the holiday season. Celebrations vary across the country in the month of December. From a traditional white Christmas in the mountains, the Ferris wheel rides and ice-skating rinks in Paris to a milder Christmas celebration on the river banks, Christmas is celebrated in style.

The first Christmas tree in France was in 1521. The French like to decorate their trees with lights, candles, nuts, and apples. A tree decorated with red apples symbolizes that Christmas is the light of the world. Nativity scenes are the most traditional and important decorations during the holiday season. Families have been handcrafting the holy figurines for the nativity scene for generations. In France, the nativity scene is called "*la crèche.*" La crèche is a beautiful arrangement of little buildings and figurines surrounding the Christmas crib. *Le Ravi,* "the delighted one," is a popular figurine; he has his arms raised in delight to welcome the baby Jesus.

In France, Advent begins on the first Sunday of the Christmas season. In France, Advent is honoured the same way as it is in many European countries. Advent is celebrated as the coming of Christ. The joyous celebrations of Christmas in many European countries make the transition into winter a brighter one.

Susan Rowsell

Advent is celebrated differently across the country. Many children count down the days of Christmas with a chocolate Advent calendar. Many families attend church on the Sundays of Advent; a candle is lit on one of the beautiful wreaths that adorn the windows of the church.

Throughout the country, celebrations vary from region to region. In some regions of France, St. Nicholas Day is celebrated on December 6th, with large parades, festive meals, and spectacular firework displays. In Lyon, France, the festival of lights is held. For four days, monuments, hills, and rivers light up in festive colours. This festival is held on December 8th, to honour the Virgin Mary.

La Veille de Noël or *le Réveillon de Noël* is the night of Christmas Eve. The festive meal is called *"le Réveillon."* The French cuisine is an elaborate assortment of foods. In the region of Provence, it is traditional to serve thirteen desserts at the end of the meal to represent Jesus and his twelve disciples. Traditional Christmas Eve feasts consist of roast turkey with chestnuts, or roast goose, oyster, lobster, venison, and lots of cheese and wine.

In some regions of France, families still burn the Yule log from Christmas Eve through to New Year's Eve to bring good luck to the family in the coming year. *La Bûche de Noël*, the Christmas log, is a traditional dessert in France.

Children leave their shoes by the fireplace on Christmas Eve for *Père Noël*.

The French bring in the coming year with a kiss under the mistletoe.

The French celebrate Three Kings' Day on January 6th, in honour of the Three Kings who followed the star of Bethlehem to find Baby Jesus. Families eat the traditional Kings cake.

Noël Neigeux, été merveilleux (snowy Christmas, wonderful summer), from France.

Susan Rowsell

December **19th**

Christmas in Finland

Hyvaa Joulua

In Finland, Christmas begins with the first day of Advent. Children get out their Advent calendars and eagerly countdown the days until Christmas. In Finland, they celebrate the three holy days: Christmas Eve, Christmas Day, and Boxing Day. In countries like Finland, Norway, Sweden, and Denmark, winter celebrations date back to Nordic times. Winters are known to get extremely cold and bitter in these countries, and celebrations help eliminate some of the dreariness that can be associated with the dark, cold days of winter. In Finland, the winter celebrations were called Kekri, named after the Finnish God of Fertility and Crops. It was a three-day celebration of feasting, singing, dancing, and praying to the Sun God. Today, Christmas in Finland is celebrated with both Christianity and Nordic roots.

During the holiday season, the Finnish busy themselves, making lots of homemade desserts and Christmas decorations. The Christmas colours in Finland are red, green, pure white, gold, and silver. Wreaths are hung on doors, and lit paper stars hang in the windows of homes. Nordic billy goats made from straw can often be seen as outdoor displays, along with gnomes, angels, snowmen, and reindeer.

Lanterns and candles are very popular in Finland; they signify light during the darkest season of the year. Lanterns and candles are often displayed in gardens, bushes, trees, and on balconies. Poinsettias and miniature junipers are often exchanged among friends during the holiday season.

Traditionally Christmas trees were brought home by sleigh on Christmas Eve morning. Papa and the children would go out to find the perfect Christmas tree, while mama prepared the dining dishes for the evening meal. It is now typical in Finland for many families to get their Christmas tree a week before Christmas. Christmas trees are decorated with paper flags, tinsel, glass balls, fruits, candies, ribbons, lights, and a golden star.

According to Finland legend, Santa Claus is known as *Joulupukki,* and he lives on the mountain of Korvatunturi in northern Finland. This is known as "Lapland." Lapland is full of reindeer. There is even a tourist park in Finland known as Santa Claus Village. This tourist park is designed to resemble Santa's village. Families enjoy visiting Santa Claus Village during the holiday season.

In Finland, even the animals take part in the holiday celebrations. It is customary for farmers to hang wheat sheaves on trees for animals. Nuts and seeds are placed in the snow. The Finnish believe in taking care of the animals in the harsh months of winter.

Christmas Eve is a very busy day in Finland. Families usually attend a very early morning church service. Some families head out to get their Christmas tree. Women are usually

Susan Rowsell

busy preparing the evening feast and baking holiday treats. In Finland, all the markets and stores close at noon. At exactly noon, the Turku Cathedral bell strikes and the "Declaration of Christmas Peace" is read and televised throughout the country. In Finland, Christmas represents a peaceful time for family and friends. It is forbidden to disrespect the peacefulness of the holiday season. After enjoying a late lunch, families enjoy an afternoon sauna bath.

At six o'clock in the evening, many family members travel to cemeteries and leave lighted candles at the graves of their family members that have passed away. Thousands of flickering lights cast a majestic glow against the snow-covered fields. The Christmas meal is an elaborate meal consisting of ham or pork roast, casseroles with carrots and rice, fish, bread, prune tarts, berry puddings, and gingerbread cookies. The Christmas drink is *glogg*, which is mulled wine.

Christmas Day is a quiet day. Families exchange gifts and cards with loved ones. They enjoy a simple meal and reflect on the serenity of the holiday season.

In Finland, New Year's Eve is the most important night of the year. Magic takes place on this special night. Cows talk and seals take on human form. The dead rise from their graves, and elves and gnomes make their way back home. There are huge bonfires and firework displays.

The Christmas season in Finland is a time of simplicity and serenity.

Greetings of peace and serenity to you and yours, from Finland.

Susan Rowsell

Christmas in Holland

Vrolijke Kerst ~ Prettig Kerstfeest

Christmas in Holland begins in late November. St. Nicholas arrives in Holland on the last Saturday of November, by steamboat, to officiate the holiday season. He parades through the streets on his grey snow horse, Amerigo, with his partner, Black Peter. Black Peter hands out candies and gingerbread cookies to all the children. St. Nicholas and Black Peter travel to the Royal Palace where children get to visit with them. It is very customary in Holland for children to be held accountable for their behaviour.

In the eastern part of Holland, families announce the arrival of Christmas from the first Sunday of Advent until Christmas Day by blowing a large horn on each of the four Sundays. Families begin decorating for the holidays in early December. Homes are trimmed with holly, candles, and evergreens. Children hang their stockings by the mantle. Christmas trees are decorated with glass balls, ribbons, sparkly pinecones, and bells. Advent stars with red and white candles are displayed in the front windows of homes. Christmas trees stand high in town squares all across the country.

During the holiday season families enjoy a traditional Holland dessert called *kerststol*. Kerststol is a loaf of bread with dried fruit, eggs, milk, and sugar incorporated into the dough, with a marzipan baked in the centre.

St. Nicholas Eve is celebrated on December 5th. This is the biggest celebration of the season in Holland. Families enjoy good food, hot chocolate, and the letter cake. The letter cake represents the family gift giving that occurs in the evening. Families enjoy a secret gift exchange. They exchange small gifts. Each gift contains a small letter that describes something nice about both the giver and the receiver of the gift. Families then try and guess who gave them their gift. Children fill their shoes with hay and place them by the fireplace before they go to bed. In the morning, they will find their shoes filled with presents and sweets.

Christmas Day is a quiet day of reflection in Holland. Families enjoy a meal of shrimp, smoked fish, eel, roast duck, or turkey and seasonal vegetables. They enjoy deep fried ice cream and pastry logs filled with sweet almond paste.

In Holland, December 26th is known as Second Christmas Day. Families usually go out for dinner and enjoy a festive musical performance.

Prettige Feestdagen—Pleasant Holidays, from Holland.

Susan Rowsell

December 20th

Christmas in Portugal

Feliz Natal

Feliz Natal from Portugal; which means "Happy Christmas." Christmas in Portugal is a festive celebration of Catholicism. During the Christmas season, towns are ablaze in holiday cheer. The Christmas tree is decorated and displayed in festive colour. It is customary that the children of the house gather the materials for the creche. The creche represents the nativity scene for the Holy Family.

Christmas Eve is the most important night of the year in Portugal. Families gather around the creche singing Christmas carols and sending blessings to God. Children write their letters to *Pai Natal*, who is Santa Claus. Baby Jesus helps Pai Natal deliver presents to the children on Christmas Eve. The *cepo de natal* is known as the Yule log, and it burns throughout the night. The *Consoada* is the Christmas feast. The feast is eaten while the children anxiously await the arrival of Pai Natal. Empty seats are placed at the table for the souls of the dead. Food crumbs are left for the souls of the dead; this is believed to bring good luck to the family in the coming year. The Christmas feast consists of boiled codfish, potatoes, and cabbage. There is a grand selection of rich desserts to be enjoyed throughout the evening. The traditional Christmas cake is known as *Bolo Rei*. It is a Christmas fruit cake with two surprises inside. One is a ring or a doll, and the other is a bean. The person who gets the bean must make the Christmas cake for the following holiday season. Many families attend the Master of the Rooster service at midnight.

Children open their presents on Christmas morning. Families enjoy a simple lunch and a sip or two of wine. Families indulge in a grand assortment of desserts.

The Christmas season in Portugal ends on January 6th, Three Kings' Day. On the eve of Three Kings' Day, children leave their shoes out to be filled with small presents and sweets by the Three Kings. Another magical Christmas season comes to an end in Portugal.

Boas Festas—Happy Holidays, from Portugal.

Susan Rowsell

Christmas in the Czech Republic

Vesele Vanoće

Christmas in Czech Republic begins on the first Sunday of Advent. Advent wreaths adorned with four candles are displayed in homes throughout the country. The children are given homemade Advent calendars to countdown the days of the holiday season. In the Czech Republic, the spirit of the holiday season comes to town on St. Nicholas Day. St. Nicholas is known as *Svaty Mikaláš*. He climbs down from Heaven on a golden rope with his companions, an angel and a devil carrying a whip. Svaty Mikaláš wears a long white robe with a red cape and carries baskets of treats for the children. The devil clanks his chains and stomps his feet, scaring young children with his devilish behaviour. The angel soothes and comforts the young ones while Svaty Mikaláš hands out presents and sweets to the children.

In the Czech Republic, Christmas is a time to celebrate the life, love, and destiny of the coming year. On December 4th, young women put cherry twigs in water. If the twig blossoms by Christmas Eve, the young women will marry in the coming year. Women should be kissed under the mistletoe during the Christmas season to ensure love in the coming year.

In the Czech Republic, families love to decorate the Christmas tree. They decorate with homemade decorations. Women spend a lot of time making perfect holiday cookies and desserts. Nativity scenes are very popular. There are families that have constructed and taken care of nativity scenes for over two hundred years. Museums are open year round to show nativity scene displays. During the Christmas season, families open their homes to visitors to show them their homemade nativity scene designs. Jan Probošt in East Bohemia had his nativity scene declared a national cultural heritage. His nativity scene has over two hundred carved components and an electrical mechanism that puts his whole scene into motion.

Christmas Eve is the most celebrated night of the holiday season in the Czech Republic. Many people fast throughout the day in hopes of seeing the golden pig in the evening. The golden pig brings good luck to families in the coming year. Christmas Eve is known as "Generous Day." It is customary to have a bountiful feast. Even the poor have a bountiful feast on Christmas Eve. Farm animals and outdoor critters are given a special treat as well. Dinner is served when the first star appears in the night sky. Carp scales are placed under the plates on the table, as they believe they will be rewarded with financial security in the coming year. Some people put scales in their wallets in belief that they will always have money in their wallet in the coming year. The bountiful feast consists of carp, potato salad and mushroom, sauerkraut, or fish soup. There are lots of homemade desserts, including Linzer cookies, which are beautifully prepared for the festive meal. During the meal, it is customary to cut an apple in half. If the seeds inside the apple form a five-pointed star, everyone at the table will be rewarded with good health in the coming year. If the apple has less than five seeds, someone will fall ill in the coming year. After dinner, families enjoy carolling by the Christmas tree. Baby Jesus leaves presents for the children.

During Midnight Mass, families listen to the "Czech Christmas Mass," composed by Jakub Jan Ryba. This composition tells the story of the birth of Jesus Christ and the arrival of the shepherds in Bethlehem. Families spend the rest of the holiday season in reflection of their good fortune and anticipate all the good tidings in the coming year.

Happy health and happy days for the coming year, from the Czech Republic.

Susan Rowsell

December 21st

Christmas in Puerto Rico

Feliz Navidad

Christmas in Puerto Rico is celebrated from late November until the middle of January. Puerto Rican homes are decorated with Christmas trees, twinkling lights, and shiny bulbs. Hooved angels are very important decorations that sit atop the Christmas tree. Gingerbread houses and nativity scenes are decorated and displayed in homes. Figurines of the Three Kings are on display in most homes across Puerto Rico.

The Puerto Ricans love to go Christmas carolling during the holiday season. They call this tradition "*parrandas*." Groups of carollers go door to door waking people up to join in the festive fun. Band members sing and play the guitar, tambourine, and the maracas. Refreshments are served. Most of these festive gatherings last until the wee hours of the morning.

The Puerto Ricans love to party over the holiday season. The *lechón asado* is another traditional celebration in Puerto Rico. A pig is put to roast at about three in the morning. People begin gathering early in the morning for this all-day party. There is lots of music and drinking. Women prepare traditional dishes. The children love to play hide and seek.

Masses are held at dawn each day from December 15th through to Christmas Eve. The Puerto Ricans enjoy large musical performances during these services.

Christmas Eve is another grand celebration for Puerto Rican families. Families enjoy a lavish meal of roast, pork, rice, and beans. The traditional dessert is called *"tembleque."* This dessert is a custard made with coconut, cornstarch, vanilla, and cinnamon. Coconut nog is the traditional holiday beverage. The majority of families attend Mass of the Rooster at midnight. Candles are aglow throughout the church service. Children act out the Christmas play.

Holy Innocents' Day is celebrated on December 28th. Much like April Fool's Day, people like to play tricks on one another. In some towns in Puerto Rico, traditional pranks are played on people. Men dress up as King Herod's soldiers and kidnap children. The children are returned when the ransom of sweets and candies has been paid. This is a prank all done in fun. However, this day is celebrated in honour of the male children that were slaughtered in Bethlehem under King Herod's order. Masses are also held on this day.

New Year's Eve in Puerto Rico is called *"Despedida de Año."* When the clock strikes midnight, it is traditional to eat one grape for each chime to ensure good luck in the coming year. There are large firework displays.

Epiphany is also celebrated by most Puerto Ricans. On Epiphany Eve, many Puerto Ricans attend mass to honour the Three Wise Men. Children leave fresh grass in their shoe boxes in hopes that the Three Wise Men will fill them with gifts and sweets.

The holiday festivities conclude with the children enjoying their holiday treasures. Christmas trees are burned, and the ashes are saved for lent. Water is thrown out windows to get rid of negative energy.

May your holiday season be filled with good luck. Merry Christmas, from Puerto Rico.

Christmas in Peru

Feliz Navidad

The first Christmas to be celebrated in Peru is believed to be in 1533. The Christmas season comes to this small South American country just as the summer season is beginning. The majority of the population is Roman Catholic, and the holiday celebrations in Peru are of a religious nature.

The people of Peru begin decorating for the holiday season the first week of December. They decorate with great flair. Families decorate their Christmas trees. Most families have a nativity scene displayed under the tree. The baby Jesus is placed in the cradle on Christmas Eve. Families like to make decorations out of pottery. Towns and cities like to display Yuletide scenes.

Christmas markets are popular during the holiday season in Peru. Families shop at the Christmas markets to purchase homemade figurines of the Holy Family for their nativity scenes. It is also traditional to place contemporary figurines from the community into their nativity scenes. The people of Peru like to honour bakers, postal workers, and store clerks.

Susan Rowsell

People like to visit family and friends during the holiday season. It is customary to bring a festive dessert when visiting. *Chancaca* and *panetón* are traditional desserts in Peru.

Christmas Eve in Peru is called *"Noche Buena."* Families attend the Mass of the Rooster at ten o'clock in the evening. Families are home by midnight and enjoy a festive feast of roasted turkey with an assortment of salads and festive desserts. Families make a toast to Baby Jesus. Gifts are left for the children by Baby Jesus or Santa Claus. All the gifts are placed in the nativity scene.

Some families celebrate Epiphany Day on January 6th. This celebration is called *"Bajada de Reyes."* A round sweet bread is baked by the women of the household. The top of the cake is decorated with a candy-shaped crown. A small figurine of Baby Jesus is placed inside the cake. The person who gets the baby Jesus figurine will have good luck in the coming year. Parents drink champaign. Children get to drink hot chocolate with cinnamon and cloves. Children receive more presents. The skies light up at midnight with spectacular firework shows. Families salsa the night away.

May your holiday season be filled with laughter and love; holiday greetings, from Peru.

Christmas in the Philippines

Maligayang Pasko

The Philippines have the longest holiday celebrations in the world. The Philippines begin singing Christmas carols in September. Legend says that the Three Wise Men saw the star that would guide them to the baby Jesus in September. Thus, the holiday celebrations kick off at the beginning of September for the Philippines. Malls stock the shelves with holiday decor. Families start their holiday shopping. The Philippines love to shop for Christmas presents. If you don't start your shopping early, you may not get to complete your shopping list.

The Philippines love to decorate. Stores, homes, businesses, and streets are all dressed up in holiday decor. The Philippines love to have holiday parties all through the holiday season. They love to sing and dance and eat and drink. They love to build up the anticipation of the holiday season. There are parties at schools and offices. There are family parties and parties with sports teams. Most of these parties have a potluck theme and many parties have secret Santa exchanges.

The *Simbang Gabi* is a long-time Philippine tradition that runs from December 16th through to Christmas Eve. Families wake up between three o'clock to five o'clock a.m. to attend mass. This is a tradition derived from early Spanish colonial times to compromise with the farmers who awoke at the break of dawn. Traditional rice cakes are served at the local Cathedrals during Mass. During mass families send blessings to the Virgin Mary.

Christmas Eve is the most important night of the Christmas celebrations in the Philippines. Christmas Eve is called *"Noche Buena."* Noche Buena is a large open house celebration. Families open their homes to friends, relatives, and neighbours. Tables are laden with food. The Philippines love to eat during the holidays. Traditional Philippines foods are cheese, sweet Christmas ham, and fruit salad. *Santa R-Kayma Klaws* visits children on Christmas Eve, leaving gifts and filling stockings. Santa R-Kayma Klaws owns the only reindeer farm in the Philippines. Many families stay up singing and dancing into the wee hours of the morning.

Christmas Day is a relaxing day, very well needed with such a long season of celebrating.

Embrace the season of Christmas from the beginning to the end. Season's greetings, from the Philippines.

Christmas in Egypt

Milad Majid

Christmas in Egypt begins on the first day of Advent, which is November 25th. Christmas ends on Christmas Day, which is January 7th. During the forty-five days of Advent, Egyptians fast. They are forbidden to eat any foods derived from animals. They cannot eat milk, fish, meat, eggs, or cheese. This fasting is called "Winter Lent fasting." Winter Lent fasting is a celebration to honour the forty days that Moses endured while receiving the ten commandments from God, and the three days associated with the miracle of moving the mountain of Mokattam. During Advent, homes are decorated with Christmas trees and lights.

The birthplace of the Christmas tree was in Egypt, long before Christmas was ever celebrated. The palm tree is known to put forth a shoot every month, and a spray of this tree with twelve shoots was used during the Winter Solstice. This tree was a symbol that another year was complete.

Susan Rowsell

Store fronts have belly dancing Santa displays. Vendors set up stands throughout Egypt where they sell blinking Santa hats. You can get your picture taken with Santa on a camel. Churches in Egypt are decorated with coloured lamps, mangers, and angels. There are Christmas markets and bazaars where shoppers can purchase their holiday gifts. A lot of the money earned at these markets is donated to charity. Throughout Advent candles are lit to honour Joseph, who burned a candle to keep Mary warm. Christmas in Egypt is less commercialized than in other parts of the world. In Egypt, the festive celebrations are all about the birth of Christ.

On Christmas Eve, the church bells ring announcing the arrival of Christmas. Families dress in their finest clothing to attend Midnight Mass. The largest church service in Egypt is held at the St. Mark's Cathedral by the Coptic Pope. During the church service, a special bread called *qurbaan* is served. This bread is decorated with a cross in the middle and surrounded by twelve dots, representing the twelve apostles of Christ.

After church services, families go home for a feast. This feast consists of roasted meats, *fattah*, rice, peas, beans, cucumber, dates, and figs. Santa Claus is known as Baba Noël, and he leaves small gifts of clothing and toys for the children on Christmas Eve.

On Christmas Day, families visit friends and neighbours. They bring with them special shortbread cookies called *kahk* and drink *shortbat*. Children are given a *El 'aidia*, a gift containing a small amount of money to buy ice cream and toys. Families also enjoy spending time at the park or going to the theatre. Christmas in Egypt is a traditionally honoured religious celebration for Christians, and this celebration is respected by the Muslims that live there.

Eid Milad Majid (Glorious Birth Feast), from Egypt.

Susan Rowsell

Christmas in Japan

Merii Kurisumasu

Christmas is not a traditional holiday in Japan. There is very little Christianity in Japan, and Christmas is not celebrated as the birth of Christ. In Japan, they celebrate December 23rd as the birth of the present Emperor.

There are two very unique customs in Japan during the holiday season. There is "*Daiku*," "the Great Nine," which refers to Beethoven's Ninth Symphony. This symphony is performed in cities all across Japan during the Christmas season. The second unique custom in Japan is the Christmas cake. Families eat the Christmas cake to pay tribute to the baking industry in Japan. With each passing year, Christmas is becoming more popular across the country, and more and more Japanese people are celebrating the holiday season with traditions of their own and traditions derived from other celebrations around the world.

Those that celebrate Christmas in Japan decorate their Christmas trees with gold paper fans, small toy dolls, paper ornaments, lanterns, and wind chimes. The most popular Christmas tree ornament in Japan is the origami swan. Christmas trees are displayed in hospitals to lift the spirits of the sick. The Japanese also love to go carolling in hospitals and retirement homes to spread Christmas cheer.

Mistletoe and evergreens are hung from ceilings in homes across the country. Tinsel and lights are hung in dance halls, cafés, and pinball parlours. The Japanese also love to decorate with flowers. An amulet is placed on front doors for good luck during the holiday season. Japanese children from all over the country exchange birds of peace in a pledge that war will never come again.

Many Japanese families enjoy a festive meal on Christmas Eve. The meal consists of roast beef, vegetables, and gravies and sauces. Other families enjoy a more conservative meal of fried chicken from the KFC franchise. Many years ago, a kindergarten teacher ordered KFC for her classroom Christmas party. The meal was delivered by jolly old Santa Claus. He created such an enthusiastic and jolly atmosphere for the children that it became a tradition in many schools across Japan. In 1974, KFC launched their first festive meal during the holiday season. It has become a popular holiday meal in Japan since the launch.

Santa Kurohsu visits the children of Japan on Christmas Eve and presents are opened on Christmas Day.

The Japanese celebrate New Year's Eve with great grandeur. They thoroughly clean their homes and dress in their finest clothing. Families march through their clean homes chasing away evil spirits that may be lingering. The father of the home throws dried beans in every corner of the home to keep evil spirits from returning. Families then travel to a Shinto shrine to get the attention of the *kami* and to seek good fortune in the coming year. New year's celebrations end with grand parades, large feasts, and spectacular firework displays.

Wishing you and yours happy days in the coming year, from Japan.

Christmas In Bulgaria

Vesela Koleda

Christmas in Bulgaria is called *Rozhdestvo Hristovo*, which means "Nativity of Jesus." Christmas in Bulgaria is a very religious holiday with many ancient customs to incorporate the coming of the new year. Towns and cities in Bulgaria are decorated with lots of colour and flair. Christmas trees are decorated with lighted candles; candles are lit to beckon the rebirth of the sun. Red, yellow, and gold are the colours used to decorate in Bulgaria; they represent sun and fire. The Sofia Christmas Market is a highly anticipated part of the festivities in Bulgaria.

St. Ignatius's Day is celebrated on December 20th. It is believed that the Virgin Mary was in labour for four days before giving birth to Baby Jesus. Households light candles on this day to commemorate Mary's strength and celebrate the anticipation of the Saviour's birth.

Christmas Eve in Bulgaria is called "Bandi Night." Families eagerly await the birth of Jesus Christ. Christmas Eve in Bulgaria marks the last night of the forty day Advent feast. The Christmas Eve feast consists of no meats and is seven, nine, or eleven dishes. There cannot be an even number of dishes served for the feast, or bad luck will be inflicted on the family in the coming year. Hay is placed under the tables to represent the Christ Child's birth. The feast consists of grains, vegetables, nuts, fruits, and wines. The food served during the Christmas Eve feast symbolizes fertility and abundance. Walnuts are a customary part of the festive feast. Bulgarian legend states that the order in which walnuts are cracked predicts the success and failure that will be endured in the coming year.

Three special breads are made and placed on the dining table during the meal. The first bread is dedicated to Christmas. The second bread is dedicated to village trade, and the third bread is dedicated to Bulgarian Christmas carollers. *Kolivo* is a traditional dish served on Christmas Eve. It is made with wheat, sugar, and walnuts. Christmas Eve pudding is made with wheat berries and honey. A special tree called *Badnik* is placed in the fireplace and burns throughout the meal, symbolizing the new birth of the sun. The oldest person in the family spreads frankincense throughout the house to rid the home of evil spirits.

Banitsa is a special bread that is baked with a coin inside. The person that eats the slice of bread with the coin will be rewarded with good fortune in the coming year. After dinner all the leftovers remain on the table. They are left for the ancestral ghosts and spirits to dine on. Christmas carollers go door to door singing carols. The singing of Christmas carols keeps evil spirits off the street during the holiday celebrations. Santa Claus is known as Grandfather Christmas. He arrives in Bulgaria at midnight. He leaves large bags of presents in the homes he visits.

On Christmas Day, families enjoy a festive meal consisting of meats, vegetables, and desserts. They sit by the fire and make wishes for the coming year. *Sooroovachka* is another tradition in Bulgaria. Children and grandchildren pat their elders on the head or back with a stick, wishing them good health and prosperity for the coming year.

The Bulgarians Christmas season ends with the coming year celebrations. They sing, dance, eat, and drink with great grandeur as they anticipate a new year of prosperity, good health, and happiness.

Happy wishes for the coming year, from Bulgaria.

Susan Rowsell

Christmas in Luxembourg

Schéi Krëschtdeeg ~ Fröhliche Weihnacten

Luxembourg is a small little country nestled in western Europe. The majority of the population is Roman Catholic. French is the official language. German is taught in schools, and people in Luxembourg speak English. Luxembourg is a cosy, multicultural little country that hosts a jubilant and cheerful season every December.

Luxembourg creates a magical winter wonderland of fun during the Advent season. There is the Winter Lights Festival, Christmas parades, concerts, and other holiday exhibits throughout the whole month of December. Children countdown the days of Advent with their chocolate calendars and families light candles on the four Sunday of Advent.

Christmas markets are very popular in Luxembourg. Vendors sell a variety of seasonal items, including baked goods, candles, crafts, and seasonal decorations. Families enjoy a cup of hot cocoa. Wooden huts can be found throughout the country where you can purchase the traditional holiday spiced wine served hot in a special collector's mug.

Kleeschen is the name given to St. Nicholas. He is seen in cities, shops and schools throughout the holiday season. He visits children and takes holiday snapshots with them.

At the beginning of December, children put their shoes in front of their bedroom doors or in the windowsill. St. Nicholas leaves a gift each night from December 1st through to the 5th.

Christmas parties are held all month long at retirement homes, schools, and sporting events. Children love singing Christmas carols and baking holiday cookies.

Christmas Eve is a night for family and celebrating the birth of Christ. Families enjoy a festive meal while the Yule log burns. Some families partake in the more ancient meal of black pudding with mashed potatoes and applesauce. Other families enjoy a more modern meal that consists of turkey and seafood and an assortment of vegetables. Families enjoy all of the traditional cookies baked by the children. They also enjoy the traditional Yule log cake. Almost all families attend Midnight Mass. Presents are delivered by the Christ Child.

On Christmas Day, gifts are exchanged and families enjoy a peaceful day of rejoicing the birth of Jesus Christ.

Schei Chreschtdeeg! Have nice Christmas days, from Luxembourg.

Figgy Pudding

Now bring us some figgy pudding, and bring it right now!

Plum pudding originated in the fourteenth century. Plum was the name used for any dry fruit. Dried fruits were used to preserve foods. Beef and mutton were mixed with raisins, prunes, wines, and spices. Grains could be added to make it a porridge. Plum pudding was eaten during fasting during the Christmas season.

In the early fifteenth century, it became known as plum porridge. The pudding was now made with a mix of meats, grains, vegetables, fats, spices, raisins, and currants. The mix was packaged like sausage and placed in animal stomachs and intestines until it was eaten.

By the end of the sixteenth century, plum pudding became sweeter as fruits became more plentiful. It was around this time that carollers began singing the famous Christmas carol "We wish you a Merry Christmas." The poor would go carolling to richer folks' homes, singing for some figgy pudding.

In 1647, the Puritans banned figgy pudding as it was known as a traditional Christmas dessert. King George the first reinstated the traditional dessert. During Victorian times, the dessert became like the one eaten today. Today, figgy pudding consists of breadcrumbs,

Susan Rowsell

eggs, brown sugar, raisins, currants, candied orange peels, nutmeg, cloves, allspice, and alcohol. Believe it or not, figs are only used occasionally. The recipe for figgy pudding became standardized in the nineteenth century.

Traditional Christmas puddings are filled with a generous portion of alcohol, usually rum and brandy. The pudding is then doused in brandy and set aflame. This Christmas pudding is time consuming to make. Preparations begin about five weeks before Christmas. But, for many Europeans, figgy pudding is an intricate and greatly enjoyed Christmas tradition.

Gingerbread Houses

There is nothing quite like the sweet aroma of ginger wafting through a home during the Christmas season. Beautifully decorated gingerbread houses, crisp gingerbread men with candy buttons, and icing stripes are enjoyed by children and adults alike during the holiday season.

In mediaeval England, gingerbread was simply preserved ginger. It wasn't until the fifteenth century that gingerbread was combined with cinnamon, molasses, and other sweet ingredients to make it an edible dessert.

Ginger root was first cultivated in ancient China. Originally ginger was commonly used for mediaeval treatment. It was also used as a spice to disguise the taste of preserved meats. Ginger was even known to be used as a concoction in the hopes of making a remedy for the plague. Even today, we use ginger as a remedy for nausea and stomach aches.

By the late Middle Ages, the Europeans modified the gingerbread formula yet again. They used the gingerbread to make hard cookies shaped like animals and kings and queens. These cookies became very popular at mediaeval fairs in England, France, Holland, and Germany. The shapes of the gingerbread cookies changed with the seasons. These elaborately decorated cookies became an elegant brand in England.

Gingerbread houses originated in Germany in the sixteenth centuries. The beautifully decorated gingerbread houses were made during the Christmas season. The popularity of gingerbread houses grew with the publishing of the story *Hansel and Gretel*.

Gingerbread arrived to the New World with English colonists. These popular cookies were sometimes used by the candidates during elections.

The largest gingerbread house to date was built in Bryan, Texas. This gingerbread house resembled a traditional home. A building permit was required to build this house. Over four thousand bricks were used, requiring 1,800 pounds of butter and 1,080 ounces of ginger.

Making gingerbread houses and cookies has become a well-known Christmas tradition across the globe. There are many different recipes used. There are contests in cities and towns all over the world. Families across the nation enjoy baking and decorating gingerbread cookies and houses. May the sweet scents of ginger and cinnamon and everything Christmas swift through your home this holiday season.

The Yule Log

May Good fortune and wellness be with you and yours in the coming year

The tradition of the Yule log is one that dates back to mediaeval times. Originally, it was a Nordic tradition associated with the Yule celebrations during the Winter Solstice. The Yule log was burned to symbolize the sun's return and the rebirth of the land.

Originally, the Yule log was an entire tree that was ceremonially brought into the home. The largest part of the tree was placed in the fire hearth, with the rest of the tree sticking out. The log was lit from the remains of the previous year. The log burned for the twelve days of Christmas. The burning of the Yule log was believed to protect the home from lightning and fire in the coming year.

In France, it was traditional for the whole family to cut down the log together. Some people believed the number of sparks from the fire represented the number of cattle and pigs that would be born in the coming year. Others believed they could read their fortunes from the sparks.

Many people would sit by the Yule fire sipping apple cider and telling ghost stories. They would watch the shadows on the wall. A headless shadow foretold death.

The burning of the Yule log became popular all across Europe. In England, they burned oak trees; in Scotland, they burned birch wood; and in France, they burned cherry wood. The French liked to douse the wood in wine to leave a fragrant smell in their home.

In some countries in the United Kingdom, people used a bunch of ash twigs instead of the Yule log. This came from a local legend that tells the story of Joseph and Mary. Joseph and Mary were so very cold when the shepherds found them. The shepherds burned twigs to keep them warm.

In Ireland, some people burn a large candle instead of the Yule log. The candles are burned on New Year's Eve and the Twelfth Night.

The ashes of the Yule log were used to help plants flourish and grow.

The Christmas Yule log is a traditional dessert in many countries, including France and Belgium. The world's largest Yule log cake was made in Shanghai in 2011. This cake was 3,503 feet in length. It took eighty pastry chefs to make this holiday cake.

Even today, many people around the world enjoy the cosy warmth from logs burning in a fireplace while gathered with their families. The soft lights of the Christmas tree aglow. The anticipation of Christmas on its way. May the warmth of the holiday season be with you and yours on the most magical night of the year.

Susan Rowsell

Merry Christmas from my country to yours

Regardless of how Christmas is celebrated from country to country, regardless of the traditions and customs unique to each culture, religion, or race, Christmas encompasses the same meaning worldwide. Christmas is the celebration of family and love.

It is the magical season each year when we wish for peace and goodwill to all mankind. It is the time of the year when we send wishes of prosperity and good health to our neighbours and friends. At Christmas, we wish for unity from nation to nation, sea to sea, and country to country. Let us all prosper in the knowledge and acceptance of all customs and traditions around our great globe.

May it never be offensive to say, "Merry Christmas" or "Happy Hanukkah." May it never be offensive to hang holiday lights or spread Christmas cheer. May it never be offensive to display a menorah or an Advent wreath in the front window of your home.

May the spirit of the season embrace us year after year. And may your Christmas bring you and your kin great comfort and great joy. Merry Christmas and God bless from my family to yours.

Happy Hanukkah, Happy Kwanzaa, and Yuletide Greetings, from my country to yours.

And to all a good night.

Susan Rowsell

Resources

Christmas Around the World-Why Christmas
https://www.whychristmas.com

https://www.tripsavvy.com

Thoughtco.
https://www.thought.co.com

https://wwwreadersdigest.ca

Timeanddate.com
https://www.timeanddate.com

CPSIA information can be obtained
at www.ICGtesting.com
Printed in the USA
BVHW021351021121
620554BV00019B/851